EXERCÍCIOS PARA FALAR MELHOR EM INGLÊS

SPEAKING ACTIVITIES

Jane Godwin Coury

EXERCÍCIOS PARA FALAR MELHOR EM INGLÊS

SPEAKING ACTIVITIES

DISAL EDITORA

© 2013 Jane Godwin Coury
Preparação de texto: Daniela Piva Reyes de Melo/ Verba Editorial
Revisão: Silvana Vieira Dibo
Capa e Projeto gráfico: Alberto Mateus
Diagramação: Crayon Editorial
Assistente editorial: Aline Naomi Sassaki
Ilustrações: Carlos Cunha

Dados Internacionais de Catalogação na Publicação (CIP)
(Câmara Brasileira do Livro, SP, Brasil)

Coury, Jane Godwin
    Exercícios para falar melhor em inglês : speaking
activities / Jane Godwin Coury. – Barueri, SP : DISAL, 2013.

    ISBN 978-85-7844-125-8

    1. Inglês – Estudo e ensino I. Título.

12-13625   CDD-420.7

Índices para catálogo sistemático:
1. Inglês : Estudo e ensino   420.7

Todos os direitos reservados em nome de:
Bantim, Canato e Guazzelli Editora Ltda.

Alameda Mamoré 911 – cj. 107
Alphaville – BARUERI – SP
CEP: 06454-040
Tel. / Fax: (11) 4195-2811
Visite nosso site: www.disaleditora.com.br
Televendas: (11) 3226-3111

Fax gratuito: 0800 7707 105/106
E-mail para pedidos: comercialdisal@disal.com.br

INTRODUÇÃO

Speaking Activities é um livro especialmente projetado para professores de inglês que querem proporcionar uma conversação eficiente para seus alunos. As 32 atividades apresentadas trazem oportunidades para a prática do aprendizado da língua, por meio do uso de estruturas gramaticais desafiadoras e de um vocabulário apropriado para discussões, dramatizações e expressões verbais em geral. As estruturas gramaticais abordam desde o *present simple* até as formas condicionais, e os tópicos de vocabulário lidam com temas como comida, música, compras, bares e assuntos controversos. O livro é destinado a estudantes brasileiros, uma vez que algumas das atividades refletem as dificuldades que eles podem ter, tais como a pronúncia correta de alguns verbos regulares no tempo passado. O livro também inclui tópicos atrativos ao público brasileiro, tais como um conto sobre a cidade de São Paulo e uma atividade sobre novelas.

As atividades podem ser usadas em aulas de conversação e são apresentadas em uma sequência que se inicia com as mais fáceis entre estas até as mais desafiadoras em termos de gramática e vocabulário. Estas atividades podem ainda servir como recursos adicionais para cursos regulares de inglês. Por exemplo, se o professor necessita de uma atividade para praticar o *past simple* ou vocabulário sobre bares, ele pode utilizar uma das atividades para tal. O material é adequado para turmas grandes ou pequenas, divididas em pares ou grupos.

NÍVEIS

Para cada atividade, um determinado nível do idioma é recomendado e os referenciais usados são baseados no Common European Framework of Reference for Languages (ver tabela abaixo), cabendo ao professor as devidas adaptações e adequações. Os níveis recomendados estão escritos acima de cada atividade como orientação para os professores.

Common European Framework of Reference for Languages
Source: www.britishcouncil.org

CEFR	General English		Academic	Professional				
Mastery **C2**		**CPE** Certificate of Proficiency in English	**IELTS**					**BULATS**
Effective Operational Proficiency **C1**		**CAE** Certificate in Advanced English		**BEC** Higher	**ILEC**	**ICFE**		
Vantage **B2**		**FCE** First Certificate in English		**BEC** Vantage				
Threshold **B1**		**PET** Preliminary English Test		**BEC** Preliminary				
Waystage **A2**	**YLE** Flyers	**KET** Key English Test						
Break- through **A1**	**YLE** Movers							
	YLE Starters							
Common European Framework of Reference for Languages	Cambridge Young Learners English Tests	General English	International English Language Testing System	Business English Certificates	International Legal English Certificate	International Certificate in Financial English	Business Language Testing Service

PARES E TRABALHO EM GRUPO

Como o objetivo de todas as atividades é a conversação, os alunos podem trabalhar em pares ou em grupos para uma comunicação mais eficaz. O professor deve procurar misturar os pares e grupos, sempre que possível, para que todos tenham a oportunidade de conversar entre si. Algumas ideias para realizar uma dinâmica de agrupar alunos são apresentadas a seguir:

- **Faça duas cópias de bandeiras** de diferentes países, por exemplo, duas cópias da bandeira do Reino Unido e duas cópias da bandeira brasileira. Distribua-as aleatoriamente e peça aos alunos para encontrar seu parceiro do mesmo país.

- **Peça aos alunos para fazer uma fila** de acordo com a sua data de nascimento. A prioridade da fila será o mês de janeiro suscessivamente até o mês de dezembro. Após este procedimento, o aluno deverá sentar-se em pares com o colega imediatamente atrás dele nesta fila.

- **Segure pedaços de barbante** e peça aos alunos para escolherem um dos fios. Em seguida, cada um deverá puxar seu barbante para encontrar seu parceiro.

- **Coloque os alunos em pares** de acordo com uma cor da roupa que os dois estejam vestindo e peça-lhes para que adivinhem por que você os colocou juntos.

- **Conte até cinco** e peça aos alunos para se levantarem e sentarem em um lugar diferente do que estavam antes. Eles executarão as atividades com a pessoa sentada a seu lado.

LEMBRANDO CADA AULA

É aconselhável que os alunos registrem o que foi abordado em cada aula. No início da aula, dê aos alunos o formulário abaixo ou escreva na lousa e sugira que eles façam anotações durante a aula. Por exemplo:

NEW WORDS
To stroll — to walk in a slow and relaxed manner

LANGUAGE CHALLENGES
It depends ~~of~~ **on** the situation
~~Have~~ **There is** a church in my street

PRONUNCIATION AND STRESS

Photograph   Photographer

É também aconselhável para o professor monitorar os alunos e corrigir erros após o exercício de conversação. O professor pode listar os erros dos alunos na planilha **LANGUAGE CHALLENGES** mostrada acima e após o término da atividade solicitar aos próprios alunos a forma correta. O professor, como no exemplo citado, escreve as palavras de forma correta na lousa. Com relação à pronúncia, o professor pode grifar a tônica forte da palavra e marcar o número de sílabas da mesma (como no exemplo PRONUNCIATION AND STRESS).

SUMÁRIO

① GETTING TO KNOW YOU
A PARTIR DE A2

Peça aos alunos para ficarem em pé e formarem dois círculos com o mesmo número de pessoas — um dentro do outro. Cada aluno do círculo interno deve ficar à frente de um outro do círculo exterior. Explique que cada aluno no círculo interno deve conversar em inglês com o outro à sua

frente fornecendo dados como nome, cidade de origem, etc. Os dois devem tentar obter o máximo de informações, tendo aproximadamente o mesmo tempo de fala. Após três minutos, fale 'stop'. Os alunos do círculo exterior devem dar um passo à direita e se posicionar em frente ao parceiro do círculo interior. Os novos pares terão assim a chance de conversar. Esse processo continua até que todos os alunos do círculo interior conversem com todos do círculo exterior. Após este procedimento, os alunos devem escrever seus nomes em uma folha de papel individual e afixar em diferentes localizações nas paredes da sala de aula. Todos devem circular pela sala e em cada folha de papel, de acordo com o nome nela escrito, escrever em inglês qualquer fato ou característica que lembre da pessoa com quem conversaram.

② FACTS ABOUT MY LIFE
A PARTIR DE A2

ESCREVA SEIS PALAVRAS E/OU NÚMEROS relacionados a sua vida na lousa.

Esses fatos correspondem a:

France › *I lived there for one year*

2 › *I have 2 children*

1994 › *I moved to Brazil*

7 › *My oldest child is 7 years old*

au pair › *I worked as an au pair in Germany*

chocolate › *Chocolate makes me sneeze*

Peça aos alunos para tentarem adivinhar o que cada palavra e/ou número representa. Esta é uma atividade em grupo que envolve toda a classe.

E.g. **Student**: *Have you ever been to France?*

Teacher: *Yes, actually I lived there for a year.*

Student: *What did you do there?*

Teacher: *I worked as an English teacher.*

Uma vez esclarecidas todas as palavras/números relativos ao professor, peça aos alunos para realizarem a mesma atividade em pares, ou seja, em uma folha de papel, ambos farão um quadro similar ao do professor e em sequência perguntarão um ao outro a respeito das palavras e números ali contidos. Finalmente, cada par poderá apresentar seu parceiro ao resto da classe, relatando em inglês as informações que acabou de obter.

⋮

③ SMALL TALK
A PARTIR DE A2

PEÇA AOS ALUNOS para imaginarem que estão em uma conferência no Reino Unido, tomando um café juntos em meio a um intervalo. Divida-os em grupos de quatro pessoas. Corte os *factfiles* ilustrados abaixo em quatro pedaços e dê a cada estudante um *factfile* sobre um determinado país.

Providencie uma cópia do *small talk game* para cada grupo. Todos os jogadores começam na posição START de uma coluna. O primeiro participante joga uma moeda. Se der 'cara', ele move uma casa. Se der 'coroa', duas casas. O aluno deverá, então, fazer a pergunta que estiver indicada na casa em que sua peça está para a pessoa à sua direita. A resposta deverá estar de acordo com a nacionalidade fictícia apresentada no *factfile* ou inventada caso não esteja no *factfile*. O jogo continua em sentido horário. Ao cair na casa *free question*, o jogador poderá fazer uma pergunta aleatória para qualquer outro participante.

FACTFILES

CANADA FACTFILE

POPULATION: approximately 34 million

CAPITAL: Ottawa

CURRENCY: 1 Canadian dollar (Can$) = 100 cents

TYPICAL FOOD: salmon, cod cakes, maple syrup desserts

NATIONAL SPORTS: ice hockey, skiing

TOURIST SIGHTS: Niagra falls, Banff, Montreal, Vancouver

USA FACTFILE

POPULATION: approximately 313 million

CAPITAL: Washington DC

CURRENCY: 1 dollar ($) = 100 cents

TYPICAL FOOD: Hamburgers and French fries, hot dogs, pancakes, baked potatoes, apple pie

NATIONAL SPORTS: American football, baseball, basketball

TOURIST SIGHTS: Niagra falls, Hollywood, Rocky mountains, The Great lakes, New York

ENGLAND FACTFILE

POPULATION: approximately 51 million

CAPITAL: London

CURRENCY: 1 pound (£) = 100 pennies

TYPICAL FOOD: fish and chips, roast beef, steak and kidney pie, ploughman's lunch, curry

NATIONAL SPORTS: football, rugby, cricket, golf, horse riding

TOURIST SIGHTS: London, Bath, Oxford, Cambridge.

AUSTRALIA FACTFILE

POPULATION: approximately 22 million

CAPITAL: Canberra

CURRENCY: 1 Australian dollar ($AUS) = 100 cents

TYPICAL FOOD: meat pie, barbecues, kangaroo tail soup

NATIONAL SPORTS: rugby, basketball, surfing

TOURIST SIGHTS: The Great Barrier Reef, Sydney, Ayers Rock

SMALL TALK GAME

As fichas estão disponíveis em tamanho maior no final do livro

④ JOB INTERVIEW
A PARTIR DE B1

COLOQUE UMA CÓPIA DO *Job Description* em uma parede da sala. Organize os alunos em pares. Em cada dupla, um aluno vai ler o texto e relatar para o parceiro (aluno A — relator); o outro irá escrever (aluno B — escritor) o que ouviu. O aluno A deve tentar decorar o que está escrito para reportar ao B. Este deve escrever o que entendeu. A dupla que terminar primeiro, com o texto correto, vence. Faça algumas perguntas sobre o texto, para orientar os alunos na atividade, por exemplo:

What is the job?

Which qualifications do you need?

Which languages do you need to speak?

JOB DESCRIPTION

You have seen a job in the newspaper for an executive at a multinational company. You need a university degree in Business Administration, at least 3 years experience working in a reputable company and need to speak English very well.

Explique aos alunos que eles irão participar de uma entrevista de emprego. Um aluno fará o papel do empregador e o outro do candidato. Em pares, o aluno A recebe o *Roleplay A* e o B fica com o *Roleplay B*. Eles devem ler e encenar seus papéis. Monitore-os, ajudando-os sempre que necessário enquanto fazem a atividade.

ROLE PLAY

ROLE PLAY A · EMPLOYER

You should ask the candidate the following questions and invent 4 more questions. Remember you need someone who has at least 3 years of work experience in a reputable company. After you have finished asking questions, ask him/her if he/she has any doubts.

What is your full name?
Where are you from?
Which qualifications do you have?
Tell me what skills you learnt at university.
What work experience do you have?
Tell me your strong points and weak points of working in a group at work.
Why do you want this job?
What hobbies do you have which make you feel relaxed?
What is your biggest achievement in life?

ROLEPLAY B · CANDIDATE

Your employer is going to interview you. You have a university degree in Business Administration and you were an Honors student. After university, you travelled around the world for 6 months. Then you got a job in a company which is not well known. After 2 years you got fired because you were not good at working in groups. You really want this job, so try to convince the employer you are the right person. You should ask him/her any questions at the end.

⑤ ALTERNATIVE LIFESTYLES
A PARTIR DE B1

DIGA AOS ALUNOS que cada um deles irá ler um texto (um sobre um morador de um barco — *Houseboat Dweller* e outro sobre uma mochileira — *Backpacker*). O aluno A deverá ler *Houseboat Dweller* e o B, *Backpacker*.

STUDENT A
HOUSEBOAT DWELLER

BACKGROUND

My name is John, I am single and I just turned 45. I am tall and have dark curly brown hair and blue eyes. I am from the southwest of England. I work as a cook in a country pub from 11am to 3pm and sometimes 6pm to 10pm.

MY ALTERNATIVE LIFE

I have made my home on a narrow boat on a canal. Some people may find it strange living on the water, but I love it. It is very peaceful and you can wake up in the morning listening to the birds singing outside. There is no problem in falling asleep as the boat is always swaying to and fro. I moor my boat near a main town, where I can get all my groceries and where there are facilities, such as a sports centre, a cinema and a theatre. My friends and relatives come to stay with me sometimes at weekends and we enjoy sitting on the bank fishing together. There is a big community of people living on houseboats near me, so you can always count on a friend for anything you need.

REASONS

I chose this lifestyle for two main reasons. First of all, because house prices in the UK are very expensive and I couldn't afford to buy a house. Secondly I wanted to leave the big city life and live as close to nature as possible.

STUDENT B
BACKPACKER

BACKGROUND
I am called Susan and I am 26 years old. I am single and I graduated from university when I was 22 years old. I am quite short and slim. I have blonde hair and green eyes. I have a degree in Modern Languages — French and Spanish. After university, I worked on the Eurostar train, which goes through the channel tunnel connecting the UK to France. I was a waitress and had to speak both French and English.

MY ALTERNATIVE LIFE
When I was 24 years old, I left my job at Eurostar and decided to see more of the world. I bought a backpack, a pair of good sneakers, some casual clothes and a round-the-world ticket. First of all, I went to the USA and ended up working as a housekeeper in a hotel in California. After that I caught a plane to South America and travelled around Brazil, Argentina and Chile. Then I went on to South Africa and worked in a McDonalds for 6 months in Johannesburg. I am currently travelling around Africa and plan to go to Asia afterwards.

REASONS
I made up my mind to set off on a huge journey like this because I was quite bored with life in the UK and wanted to experience different cultures and see how people live. It is completely different from being a tourist.

Coloque os seguintes tópicos na lousa para que os alunos façam anotações e posteriormente perguntas para seu/sua parceiro/a:

Name
Age
Family
Physical appearance
Job/Studies
Alternative lifestyle
Why he/she chose his/her lifestyle

Exemplos de perguntas:
What is his/her name?
How old is he/she?

Após os pares terem respondido as questões, disponibilize as seguintes frases para discussão com toda classe:

Would you like to have a lifestyle like either of these people?

What are the advantages and disadvantages of each lifestyle?

Do you know anyone who has an alternative lifestyle?

⑥ REGULAR VERBS IN THE PAST
A PARTIR DE B1

EXPLIQUE QUE EXISTEM apenas três possibilidades de se pronunciar a terminação ´ed´ dos verbos regulares no passado: /d/, /t/ e /id/. Cada aluno deve receber um *Regular verbs in the Past worksheet* e colocar os verbos na coluna adequada. Corrija as respostas (abaixo) e faça-os praticar a pronúncia. Em pares, os estudantes discutem o primeiro tópico tentando usar os verbos — *A learning curve you experienced*. Após 3-4 minutos, diga *CHANGE*. Os alunos deverão levantar-se e sentar-se em outro lugar para formar um novo par e discutir o tópico seguinte. Esta dinâmica deve ser repetida para cada tópico.

RESPOSTAS
PRONUNCIATION OF REGULAR VERBS IN THE PAST

	/d/	/t/	/id/
asked		✓	
believed	✓		
called	✓		
closed	✓		
developed		✓	
enjoyed	✓		
hated			✓
kissed		✓	
liked		✓	
loved	✓		
opened	✓		
painted			✓
showed	✓		
talked		✓	
watched		✓	
washed		✓	
worked		✓	

REGULAR VERBS IN THE PAST

Put these verbs into the different columns according to their sound and looking at the rules below

	/d/	/t/	/id/
asked			
believed			
called			
closed			
developed			
enjoyed			
hated			
kissed			
liked			
loved			
opened			
painted			
showed			
talked			
watched			
washed			
worked			

Generally, if a word in its present form ends in:

e, n, y, l, w	it has the /d/ sound
k, ss, sh, ch, p	it has the /t/ sound
t, te, d	it has the /id/ sound

Now talk to a partner using as many verbs as possible about the following topics:

1 *A learning curve you experienced*	**4** *An interesting person you met*
2 *A film you watched recently*	**5** *Your first boyfriend/girlfriend*
3 *A trip you went on*	**6** *A great TV program you watched*

FONTE: BASEADO EM UMA ATIVIDADE PREPARADA POR KAREN BOND

⑦ LIFE CYCLE
A PARTIR DE B1

DESENHE O LIFECYCLE NA LOUSA e dê a cada aluno uma cópia de *useful vocabulary*. Explique que os números em volta do *lifecycle* correspondem a diferentes idades. Os alunos se dividem em pares. Um será o *teller* e o outro, o *listener* (veja tabela a seguir). O *teller* deverá, então, escolher uma idade em particular e falar sobre suas experiências nessa época para o *listener*. Ambos devem usar o vocabulário dado na tabela trocando de papéis ao terminarem. Por exemplo: **Teller** — *did I tell you about the time when I was 5 years old and I fell off my bicycle.* **Listener** — *No, tell me about it.*

Outros pares devem ser formados e cada aluno deve recontar o que lembra sobre o parceiro inicial.

USEFUL VOCABULARY

Teller	Listener
Did I tell you about the time when...?	No, tell me about it
	Really?
You'll never guess what!	I can't believe it! You did what?
The funniest experience I've ever had was...	Wow! That's amazing!
Then/After that....	It sounds really great/bad
The best/worst part was...	Yeah, then what happened?
It was such a good laugh	It must have been hilarious!
It was awful!	God! What a nightmare!
What was really strange/ weird was...	So, what did you do?
Finally....	What happened in the end?

LIFECYCLE

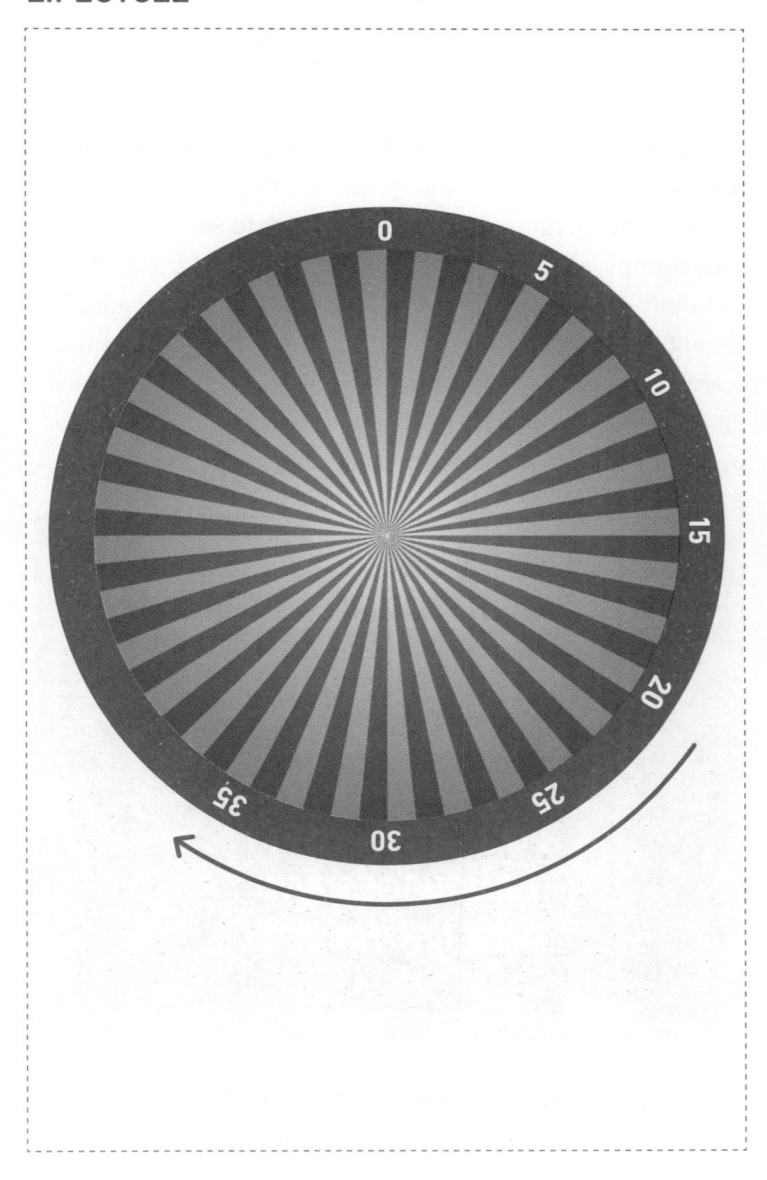

⑧ MILESTONES IN MY EDUCATION/CAREER
A PARTIR DE B1

Desenhe uma linha na lousa e escreva algumas datas marcantes na sua educação e carreira. Peça aos alunos para lhe fazerem perguntas sobre o que aconteceu nesses anos. Por exemplo: *What happened in 1992?* Resposta: *I graduated from university. I got a degree in Languages and then I got a job.* Os alunos desenham, então, uma linha e adicionam datas relevantes de suas vidas. Em pares, tendo em mãos o *Milestones in my Education and Career worksheet*, eles devem fazer perguntas e usar as frases em suas respostas.

Outros pares devem ser formados e cada aluno deve re-contar o que lembra sobre o parceiro inicial.

MILESTONES IN MY EDUCATION/CAREER

My earliest memory of school was...

When I was at elementary school I remember + ing...

When I went to high school, I felt...

I first started getting interested in ... when I was ... years old.

I spent ... years studying for my university entrance exam.

I studied all kinds of subjects including...

I got into university when I was ... years old

I got/I am studying for a degree in (*subject*)...

I did/I am doing work experience at (*place*)...

Our graduation ball was amazing/a disaster/interesting because...

My happiest memory of university was...

Afterwards, I did a Master's/PhD in...

I got a job at (*the place*) in (*the year*).

I had to do a lot of interviews and I was short listed to 6 candidates.

Luckily, I got a job as a (*profession*)

Looking back, I think...

⑨ IRREGULAR VERBS
A PARTIR DE B1

OS ALUNOS RECEBERÃO E PREENCHERÃO uma tabela de *Irregular Verbs*. Escreva as respostas na lousa. Comece uma história (no passado) usando um dos verbos. Por exemplo: *One day, a middle aged man got up and **heard** a strange noise...*

A atividade se desenvolve com cada aluno continuando a história, utilizando um dos verbos da tabela. Tique os verbos na lousa até que todos sejam incluídos.

RESPOSTAS
IRREGULAR VERBS

Verb	Past simple
begin	began
break	broke
buy	bought
catch	caught
choose	chose
drink	drank
eat	ate
fly	flew
forget	forgot
hear	heard
know	knew
leave	left
meet	met
pay	paid
read	read
say	said
speak	spoke
tell	told
think	thought
understand	understood

IRREGULAR VERBS

Verb	Past simple
begin	
break	
buy	
catch	
choose	
drink	
eat	
fly	
forget	
hear	
know	
leave	
meet	
pay	
read	
say	
speak	
tell	
think	
understand	

⑩ GROUP DYNAMIC
A PARTIR DE B2

APRESENTE A SEGUINTE SITUAÇÃO aos alunos: você é o dono de uma empresa e irá selecionar possíveis candidatos para um cargo. Os alunos vão fazer parte de uma dinâmica em grupo para conquistar a vaga. Separe-os em trios.

Em seguida, desenhe um balão de ar quente na lousa e um pássaro bicando o balão. Explique que a aeronave está prestes a cair e somente uma pessoa poderá se salvar.

Cada aluno deve pensar e personificar uma pessoa famosa, levando em conta os argumentos para que ela permaneça no balão. Eles têm cinco minutos para fazer algumas anotações e tentar convencer os demais sobre a importância de se salvarem. Em seus grupos, os participantes discutem e decidem quem poderá permanecer no balão. Coloque as seguintes frases na lousa para serem usadas durante a discussão.

In my opinion...

Personally speaking...

In my view...

I believe/think...

I must stay in the balloon because...

I should remain here owing to the fact that...

I strongly believe...

You should keep me in the balloon due to the fact that...

I don't think he/she has a valid reason because...

⑪ PEOPLE DESCRIPTION
A PARTIR DE B2

CADA ALUNO DEVE RECEBER uma cópia de *People Description* para ler. Corte várias fotos de pessoas diferentes em revistas e dê uma delas para cada aluno. Eles não devem mostrar as fotos para os outros. Peça aos alunos para escreverem a descrição da aparência física da pessoa na foto e suas roupas, usando palavras da lista *People Description*. Lembre-os de usar o *present continuous*, *e.g. She is wearing a checked shirt*. Junte todas as imagens e as redistribua a alunos diferentes. Escolha alguém da classe para descrever oralmente as anotações de sua foto original. O participante que tiver a foto descrita deve mostrá-la.

OPÇÃO
Dê a cada aluno uma cópia de *People Description* e peça-os para ler. Escolha uma cena de um filme que tenha várias pessoas. Em pares, peça ao aluno A para virar de costas para à televisão e ao aluno B para ficar em frente à televisão. Mostre a cena sem som. O B deve descrever as pessoas na cena usando as palavras da lista *People Description*. O A faz anotaçoes do que o B fala e reporta para o resto da sala. Em seguida, eles trocam de lugar e repetem a atividade usando outra cena.

PEOPLE DESCRIPTION · PHYSICAL APPEARANCE

He/She has got	light dark jet fiery	blonde brown black red grey	HAIR
He/She has got	short long straight curly wavy		HAIR
He/She has got	piercing emerald dark hazel	blue green brown coloured	EYES
He/She is	white/black quite tall/short lanky plump slim skinny barefoot		
He/She has got	striking features high cheek bones a pale/dark/olive complexion		
He/She looks like	a model an American/a Brazilian a nice person he/she is in her twenties a talkative person a shy person		
He/She looks	friendly/unfriendly healthy/fit kind well dressed/scruffy old/young stressed-out strikingly handsome (man) extremely beautiful (woman)		

PEOPLE DESCRIPTION · CLOTHES

She is wearing	a blouse
	a top
	a T-shirt
	a skirt
	a dress
	a pair of trousers/jeans
	a jumper/sweater
	a coat/jacket
	a pair of tights/socks
	a bra
	a bikini
	a swimsuit
He is wearing	a shirt
	a T-shirt
	a pair of trousers/jeans
	a jumper/sweater
	a suit
	a tie
	a coat/jacket
	a pair of Boxer shorts
	a pair of socks
	a pair of pyjamas

FOOTWEAR

He/She is wearing a pair of shoes	sneakers
	sandals
	high heeled shoes
	flip flops
	slippers

ACCESSORIES

He/She is wearing	a pair of glasses
	a hat/cap
	a scarf
	a pair of gloves

ADJECTIVES

striped/checked/spotted/flowery/dark brown/light green/lovely/
cool/horrible/disgusting.

⑫ AN UNUSUAL DAY
A PARTIR DE B2

ESTA ATIVIDADE COMEÇA COM OS ALUNOS falando sobre suas experiências da cidade de São Paulo. Peça a eles para lerem a primeira parte de *An Unusual Day*. Em pares, eles recontam a história e discutem seus desdobramentos prováveis. Ajude-os com possíveis problemas de vocabulário sempre que necessário. Após lerem a segunda parte da história, eles checam suas versões.

AN UNUSUAL DAY

São Paulo is a huge city in the Southeast of Brazil, which spreads out over miles in every direction. If you are looking out the window on the top floor of one of its many tall skyscrapers, you will see many different buildings of various shapes and sizes and people bustling here, there and everywhere. It is a modern and dynamic city where business deals take place seven days a week in posh offices and expensive restaurants all over the city.

Maiara is one of Sao Paulo´s 18 million inhabitants. Although she lives in this busy metropolis, she was not born here. She is from a nearby city called Campinas and her parents still live there. Maiara is tall, slim and has dark wavy hair which is shoulder length. She has been married to José for six years.

Every morning, Maiara wakes up at 5am when her alarm clock goes off. After having a long warm shower, she makes some strong coffee and lays the table for breakfast. José normally joins her for the first meal of the day and they usually eat papaya with honey and a bread roll with cheese. At around 6am, José kisses his wife goodbye and goes to work by car. It takes him an hour to arrive at his company as there are often intense traffic jams at this time of day.

Maiara also sets off for work. She is a helicopter pilot and works for a company which provides helicopter shuttle services from a suburb called Tamboré to many places in the centre of São Paulo. Her clients are successful businessmen and women who are smartly dressed and carry leather briefcases.

It was a sunny Tuesday morning and Maiara drove to work as normal and left her Fiat Uno in the parking lot next to the heliport in Tamboré. After greeting her colleagues, she met her client and took him to the helicopter she was to use that day. She noticed that her client was carrying a strange black box. When they got to the helicopter, they sat down next to each other and Maiara went through the pre--flight checking procedure before taking off. Everything seemed to be fine.

At 8am, the helicopter rose up over the buildings and Maiara headed in the direction of Avenida Paulista where her client, a rather chubby man with a dark moustache, had an important meeting at a multinational company. His name was Fernando Silva and he was from Angola. He had told Maiara that he was just visiting Brazil on business. They had few problems communicating as they both speak Portuguese. As they were chatting, Maiara thought that she could hear a hissing noise. However, it soon stopped and she forgot about it.

On top of some of Sao Paulo´s tall office towers are numbers which indicate where helicopter pilots must land. Maiara had been told by radio that she must go to Helipad 167, which was the headquarters of a company called Rainer. Maiara circled around the tower and gently lowered the helicopter until it stopped on top of the roof of the building. Fernando jumped out of the helicopter and said goodbye to her in a thick Angolan accent. Maiara waved at him as she lifted the helicopter off the ground.

As she was flying back, she suddenly realised that her passenger had left the strange black box on the seat beside her.

Tell the story so far to your partner. Discuss what will happen next and how the story will finish.

Maiara wondered what to do. If she turned back now, it would be dangerous to suddenly change course. She may cause an accident by doing that. She decided to go on her way and ring her passenger when she arrived back at the heliport.

She dialled the number, but there was only an answering machine so she left a message.

"Senhor Silva. This is Maiara, your helicopter pilot. I am calling to say you left your belongings in the helicopter. Please ring me."

Maiara put the box inside a safe in the company's office. Having woken up early and eaten her breakfast some hours ago, she thought it was time for a coffee and a cheese bun so she went to the heliport café to buy one. Just as she sat down to enjoy her mid-morning snack, her mobile phone rang. She picked it up and said:

"Hello."

"Maiara. This is Fernando Silva. Thanks for your message. I don't know what to do. I need the box I left in the helicopter, as there is something very important inside. Can you fly back to Avenida Paulista and bring me it? I will pay you for your services, of course".

"OK, Senhor Silva. I'll check with my boss. I don't think there will be any problem."

Maiara got the go-ahead from her boss and was soon flying back the same way she had previously flown some hours ago. Fernando's box was on the seat next to her. By this time, she was really quite curious to know what was inside it.

Maiara landed on the tower and saw Fernando waiting anxiously for her. He came running over to her and thanked her for coming all this way. After paying her for the extra trip, he turned round to go back to the door leading to the stairs of the building.

"Senhor Silva," Maiara called out. "Just one thing! Could you please tell me what is inside your box. I am a bit of a busybody or should I say curious!"

"Well, ok. Please do not tell anyone though." Fernando opened the strange black box slowly and Maiara saw a 20cm bright green snake. It had been eating a small lizard which was lying dead next to the snake.

"This is a rare snake from Angola", explained Fernando. "I am taking it to this company to show them. In fact, they are interested in buying it. I had to transport the snake in an inconspicuous way as it would have looked too suspicious."

Now, Maiara understood what the hissing sound was!

⑬ SOAP OPERA
A PARTIR DE B2

EM PARES, OS ALUNOS RECEBEM a planilha *Soap opera* e preenchem a tabela referente a cada figura usando sua imaginação. A seguir, eles discutem qual seria a provável relação entre as pessoas se elas fossem personagens de uma novela. Usando os três títulos abaixo, os pares inventam três episódios relatando os acontecimentos.

SOAP OPERA
For each picture fill in the following information:

Name
Age
Marital status
Profession
Interests

Name
Age
Interests

Name
Age
Marital status
Profession
Interests

Name
Age
Marital status
Profession
Interests

In pairs, decide what the relationship between the people is. Write your ideas here.

_____

_____

Now invent three episodes of a Soap Opera using the following titles.

A lucky day

A misunderstanding involving a mobile phone

A disastrous holiday

⑭ EXCHANGE PROGRAMME
A PARTIR DE B2

DIGA AOS ALUNOS QUE DOIS ingleses irão passar duas se-
manas em sua cidade. Os estrangeiros têm aproximadamente 25 anos e estão interessados em aprender o máximo
possível sobre o seu país. Em pares ou grupos, os alunos
discutem uma possível programação para este período.
Eles deverão falar sobre os seguintes tópicos, que podem
ser escritos na lousa:

> › Restaurants
> › Shopping
> › Leisure activities
> › Tourist sights
> › Transport
> › Advice you would give about customs

Ao terminarem, os alunos mostram seus planos para o resto da classe e votam no programa mais viável. O grupo com o maior número de votos vence. Para finalizar, eles discutem qual seria um programa ideal se estivessem na Inglaterra.

⑮ THE MYSTERY OBJECT
A PARTIR DE B2

Escreva as seguintes palavras na lousa: *garden, object, telephone*. Os alunos tentam adivinhar o tema de uma história baseando-se nas palavras sugeridas.

Peça a eles para lerem a primeira parte de *The Mystery Object*. Em pares, eles devem recontar a história e discutirem os desdobramentos prováveis. Ajude-os com possíveis problemas de vocabulário sempre que necessário. Após lerem a segunda parte da história, eles devem checar suas versões.

THE MYSTERY OBJECT

Abigail liked getting up late. She taught Spanish evening classes to adults and normally went to bed late. On this particular day she was awoken by her young neighbours who were playing music very loudly. This was normal on a Friday in the street where she lived in Southampton. There were many student houses nearby and Friday at 11am was party time for them.

Abigail, who was in her thirties, got out of bed and stretched her arms. She brushed her long dark hair and went downstairs to make herself some breakfast. She put a bowl of cornflakes and a carton of milk on the table. Then, she sat down on her favourite chair still feeling half asleep. There was a local newspaper on the table. She hadn't had time to read it yesterday so she started flicking through the pages. Suddenly, she saw something that caught her eye on page six. There was a person in a picture that she recognised. Underneath the picture, there was an article. It went like this:

Edward Banks, a landscape designer from Lymington, decided to remodel his garden. This 42-year-old man wanted to plant some apple trees and so he dug some holes in his back garden. While he was digging, he came across something hard.

He said "Luckily I didn't break the object. I knew it must have been something precious as I could see a shining gold color gleaming from the ground."

Edward tried to make a bigger hole and felt the object with his hands. At that very moment, his telephone rang and he hurried quickly into the house to answer it. When he picked up the phone, there was no-one there.

"I thought it was strange," exclaimed Edward.

He put the phone down and went back outside. When he got to the hole, he looked inside and noticed that there was no golden colored object there anymore.

Abigail was very interested in the story and wanted to know the end. She became very frustrated, though, when she realized that the end of the story was missing. Her dog, Rover, had picked up the newspaper and had chewed up a piece of it. She was very curious to know what had happened to Edward.

Tell the story so far to your partner. Discuss what will happen next and how the story will finish.

Abigail thought for a moment about where she had met Edward.

"Now I remember," she said out loud. "He was in my cooking class I took last year at college."

She tried to visualize what he looked like. A picture came to mind of a tall man who had blond hair. During the course at college, the students had exchanged phone numbers. Abigail got her notebook that she had used at that time and found Edward's number. She decided to ring her former classmate to see what had happened.

They arranged to meet up at a nice café on King's Road the following Saturday. Both Abigail and Edward arrived on time and were pleased to see each other again. Edward told Abigail the story that she had already read in the newspaper. He added that he had ended up in hospital that day because he'd got very anxious about the whole story and had experienced a nervous breakdown. He had told his family and friends about what had happened in the garden but no one had believed him.

Abigail asked Edward if he would like to look for the object again. She would help him if he agreed. Edward was very happy because someone finally believed him. They went back to his house and Edward found two spades, one for him and one for Abigail. They started digging.

"Look!" yelled Abigail suddenly. "I've found something."

Edward quickly rushed over to see what she had discovered. It was a yellowish box with a hole in it. They both pulled it out of the ground. Inside the hole, there was a piece of paper with a plastic bag wrapped around it. By this time, Edward and Abigail were very excited.

"You open it," suggested Edward.

"OK," Abigail said tearing the plastic bag. The piece of paper was a little brown, but they could still read it. It said:

Pupils from St. John's School in Southampton buried this box on 23th March, 1965.
Whoever finds it will see 3 things that reflect our life at the time of writing.

1 a cassette of the Beatles

2 a mini skirt

3 a Beatles wig

Edward looked at Abigail and they both burst out laughing. What a pity they didn't have a cassette player!

⑯ WHAT WOULD YOU DO?
A PARTIR DE B2

CORTE AS SITUAÇÕES DA PLANILHA *What would you do?* e as coloque em um monte voltadas para baixo. Divida os alunos em grupos de 3. Peça a cada um deles para ler em voz alta uma situação e responder à pergunta. As outras pessoas do grupo devem expressar a sua opinião.

WHAT WOULD YOU DO?

1 *Imagine you are walking down the road, when you see someone being pick-pocketed. What would you do?*	**2** *You are in a foreign country and your host serves a strange looking dish. When you ask what it is, he says it is pig's eyes — a delicacy. What would you do?*
3 *You go to a conference and your power point presentation does not work. What would you do?*	**4** *You see your friend's husband having a romantic dinner with a woman in a restaurant, who is not his wife. What would you do?*
5 *You go to a beach with your friend and when you arrive you find out it is a nudist beach. What would you do?*	**6** *You receive an invitation through the post to take part in a reality show on TV. What would you do?*

7 *You have invited your parents-in-law for dinner and in the middle of the meal, a cockroach crawls across the table. What would you do?*

8 *You dye your hair black for a fancy dress party. When you wash it the next day, your hair goes green! What would you do?*

9 *A native speaker tells a joke in English and you don't get it. What would you do?*

10 *You find £100 in the bathroom at an airport. What would you do?*

11 *You buy something in a shop and notice that the cashier has shortchanged you for a product. What would you do?*

12 *You share a house with 3 other people. You open the fridge and it stinks of a French cheese that your friend bought on vacation. What would you do?*

13 *Your colleague has terrible B.O. (body odour) and it is bothering you. What would you do?*

14 *You notice that your colleague is wearing one red sock and one blue one. What would you do?*

15 *In a meeting your boss tells everyone some information that you know is incorrect. What would you do?*

16 *You are on holiday in a foreign country and you park in a no parking zone. You get a parking ticket. What would you do?*

17 *Your friend wins a free makeover at a department store. When you see her, you think she looks awful. What would you do?*

18 *You borrow a book from your English teacher and on the way home it gets sopping wet. What would you do?*

19 *You have invited a foreigner to your home for a meal. At the end of the meal, he burps. What would you do?*

20 *You buy a car from a second hand dealer who assures you the air conditioning is working. After you have bought it, you find out there is no air conditioning! What would you do?*

⑰ PARTY POOPERS
A PARTIR DE B2

CORTE A PLANILHA PARTY POOPERS e divida as cartas em *Profiles* e *How to deal with this person*. Em pares, os alunos recebem e analisam as características das pessoas contidas no *Profile*, comentando sobre possíveis conhecidos com este perfil.

Em seguida, eles discutem como lidariam com esses tipos de pessoas em uma festa. Distribua as cartas de *How to deal with this person* e peça para eles formarem os pares com os *Profiles* correspondentes. Finalmente, proponha uma discussão comparando as respostas originais com as sugeridas nas cartas.

PARTY POOPERS

PROFILE • THE CRITIC
Nothing you do is good enough. This person's comments always provoke you or initiate competition. Typical things he/she says are ´*the turkey is delicious but you have been so overworked that I think you left it too long in the oven*´ or *Christmas at so and so´s house was much better last year. She is a great hostess*´ and so on.

HOW TO DEAL WITH THIS PERSON

The best way is to let him/her feel important. For example, in the case of the turkey, say that your turkey is not as good as his/hers and ask for their advice to improve the recipe. Asking for co-operation is always a good way of avoiding competition. People who are like this, need to be recognized. They need approval from people for things they do.

PROFILE • THE DRUNK

The more they drink, the more intense they get. They start hugging people, crying and giggling. Sometimes they even want to tell rude jokes that don't go down very well and no one finds them funny.

HOW TO DEAL WITH THIS PERSON

Keep cool. If you get offended by anything they say, the party could end up in a fight. If you are the hostess/host and notice that this person is annoying the other guests, discretely lead them away and take them somewhere else. Don't think about hiding the booze as this could cause the person to get angry. If you don't want drunk people at your party, don't serve alcohol.

PROFILE • THE HYPOCHONDRIAC

This person goes on and on about their illnesses and they talk in detail about the medicine they are taking. A conversation with them goes something like this *'today I woke up with a terrible pain in my side. Do you think it is serious? They say that this is a symptom of bird flu. Yesterday I had a backache and took some medicine and I think my liver has been affected now. I took something else for my liver and then I almost died of stomachache. Do you think I am going to get bird flu?'*

HOW TO DEAL WITH THIS PERSON

Be patient. This kind of person is normally an attention seeker. If the conversation gets too unbearable say "*now tell me something good that's happening in your life.*" Try to get them to talk about positive things. Try not to be sucked into their world and start saying "*Oh me too*" as this may lead to a competition of who is the worst victim!

PROFILE • THE LAZY GUY

He/She always arrives late and empty handed. Other people's houses are an extension of their own, which means they feel free to meddle with your things, wee in your bathroom with the door open or lie down on the sofa with their shoes on. They will probably ask for more tea or cake while lounging on the sofa and they never offer to clean up.

HOW TO DEAL WITH THIS PERSON

Say "*Please feel free to get a piece of cake yourself. It's in the kitchen.*" By doing this you won't be at their beck and call all the time. If you are upset about them meddling with your things, close the door of the room where you want privacy. Hide things you don't want visitors to touch or see. If you want them to help, ask. For example you could say "Could you please put your dirty cup in the kitchen and when they are in the kitchen, hand them a tea towel and ask them to dry up."

PROFILE • THE GOSSIPER

They know sordid details about everyone's lives and don't miss a chance to gossip about someone. They have an intense morbid pleasure in exposing people's secrets.

HOW TO DEAL WITH THIS PERSON

Try not to listen to gossip and discretely leave. If there is no way out, listen quietly without making comments which can be used against you. Do not repeat anything you heard as this only spreads gossip. If it involves anyone who is there, call the person over to take part in the conversation and find out if it is true.

⑱ ADOPTING A CHILD
A PARTIR DE B2

CONTE A SEGUINTE HISTÓRIA e peça aos alunos para dese-
nharem a situação ali contida:

*A truck driver was in a gas station and was just about to get into
his truck when he heard a baby crying. He looked under his lorry
and saw a one-week old baby boy screaming right in front of his
wheel. He picked the baby up and took him to the authorities.
Now the baby is up for adoption and the authorities are looking
for the ideal parents.*

Após compararem os desenhos, os alunos recebem a planilha *Adopting a Child*. Peça para que, individualmente, eles chequem a lista de critérios para adoção, marcando cada item na escala de 1 (muito importante) a 5 (não importante).

Em grupos de 3, eles discutem cada item, usando as frases (*agreeing and disagreeing*) para apresentar seus argumentos.

ADOPTING A CHILD

A truck driver was in a service station and was just about to get into his truck when he heard a baby crying. He looked under his truck and saw a one-week old baby boy screaming right in front of his wheel. He picked the baby up and took him to the authorities. Now the baby is up for adoption and the authorities are looking for the ideal parents.

Mark each item of the list of criteria below on a scale of 1 (very important) to 5 (not important at all). Then, get into groups of 3 and discuss each point. Use the agreeing and disagreeing phrases in your discussion.

CRITERIA

The ideal parents should:
- ❏ be under 30 yrs old
- ❏ be of the same racial group as the child
- ❏ be of the same religious group as each other
- ❏ be a married couple
- ❏ be a heterosexual couple
- ❏ both have jobs
- ❏ have other children in the family
- ❏ not be living in poverty
- ❏ have some professional experience of dealing with children, i.e. as teachers or nurses

Agreeing	Disagreeing
I completely agree with you.	I don't agree with you at all.
I agree with your point of view.	No way could I agree to that (informal)
I think you're right.	I respect your opinion, however...
By and large, I would accept what you just said (formal)	I am not totally convinced by what you said.
Exactly, I feel the same way.	I really must take issue with you here (formal)
I agree up to a point, but...	We'll have to agree to disagree then.

⑲ THE BEATLES
A PARTIR DE B2

Comece perguntando aos alunos seus conhecimentos sobre os *Beatles*. Divida-os em pares, e peça-os para completarem *The Beatles Quiz*. Em seguida, eles checam suas respostas lendo o texto *THE BEATLES*.

ANSWERS
1b, 2c, 3a, 4b, 5a, 6b, 7b.

Uma canção dos *Beatles* pode ser usada no final para complementar essa atividade.

THE BEATLES QUIZ

1 Where were the Beatles from?
a London
b Liverpool
c New York

2 What was the name of John Lennon´s first group?
a The Beat up
b The Beetles
c The Quarrymen

3 Who thought of the name The Beatles?
a John Lennon
b Paul McCartney
c George Harrison

---

4 Which song was The Beatles first UK hit?
a Lucy in the Sky with Diamonds
b Love me Do
c Yesterday

5 Which country did The Beatles go to in 1968 to learn about meditation?
a India
b Tibet
c The USA

6 When did the Beatles split up?
a 1969
b 1970
c 1971

7 How did John Lennon die?
a He died of cancer
b He was shot
c He died in a car accident

THE BEATLES

The Beatles were an English group from Liverpool who continue to be held in tremendously high esteem for their artistic achievements. The innovative music and style of John Lennon (1940-1980), Paul McCartney (1942-), George Harrison (1943-2001) and Ringo Starr (1940-) helped to define the 1960's.

In March, 1957 John Lennon formed a group called The Quarrymen. On 6th July of that year, Lennon met Paul McCartney while playing at the Woolton Parish Church Fete. In February, 1958, the young guitarist George Harrison joined the group, which was then playing under a variety of names. A few primitive recordings of Lennon, McCartney and Harrison from that era have survived. During this period, members continually joined and left the line up. Lennon, McCartney, and Harrison were the only constant members. Ringo Starr joined them in 1962.

The origin of the name "The Beatles" — with its unusual spelling — is usually credited to John Lennon, who said that the name was a combination word-play on the insects "beetles" as a nod/compliment to Buddy Holly´s band (The Crickets) and the word "beat". In addition to being a fan of the Crickets, Lennon is paraphrased as having said: "if you turn it round it was "les beat," which sounded French and cool".

In September, 1962, the Beatles produced a UK hit "Love Me Do", which charted. (Love Me Do reached the top of the U.S. singles chart over 18 months later in May 1964). This was swiftly followed by the recording of their second single "Please Please Me". Three months later they recorded their first album (also entitled Please Please Me), a mix of original songs by Lennon and McCartney with some covers of their favourite songs. The band's first televised performance was on a program called *People and Places* transmitted live from Manchester on 17th October, 1962.

The Beatles´ music changed styles throughout the years. In the beginning, they were heavily influenced by Rock and Roll. Later, Lennon played a major role in steering The

Beatles towards psychadelia. Some of their music was inspired by classical music such as the music of Bach. In 1968, the group spent the early part of the year in India, studying transcendental meditation and they used an Indian instrument called the sitar in many songs.

The Beatles split up when Paul McCartney said he was leaving the band in April, 1970, and on 31st of December, 1970, the band officially broke up. All four Beatles went on to have very successful solo careers with Paul McCartney, now Sir Paul, still recording and performing.

Sadly, on 8th of December, 1980, John Lennon was going back to his flat in New York when he was shot dead by a fan who wanted him to autograph a record. In 1999, George Harrison survived a stabbing after an intruder broke into his house. But on 29th of November, 2001, he died after a long battle against cancer.

The Beatles are known for being the most popular band in the world. You can be pretty sure that if you ask someone in any country, they have heard of them.

FONTE: WWW.BBC.CO.UK

⑳ MAKE AND DO GAME
A PARTIR DE B2

FAÇA DUAS COLUNAS NA LOUSA, uma com MAKE e outra com DO. Cheque as expressões que os alunos possam saber usando MAKE e DO e escreva-as na lousa. Por exemplo: *make a phone call, do business.* Dê uma cópia do *Make and Do game* e um set de cartas para cada grupo de quatro alunos.

Coloque as *Make and Do cards* viradas para baixo na mesa com o jogo. Você precisará de um pino e um dado. Todos usam o mesmo pino. A primeira pessoa joga o dado e move o pino de acordo com o número mostrado. Quando parar no espaço com uma estrela, o participante deverá pegar uma carta e perguntar à pessoa na sua direita a questão indicada, usando a palavra correta — MAKE ou DO. Peça aos alunos para anotarem as expressões que aparecem durante o jogo em duas colunas — MAKE ou DO. Ao cair em um espaço com uma palavra escrita, o jogador deverá usá-la em uma frase com MAKE ou DO. A próxima pessoa joga o dado e usa o mesmo pino no sentido horário e assim por diante. O jogo termina quando todos os espaços forem respondidos.

RESPOSTAS
MAKE AND DO GAME

Ask someone how often they do the housework	Ask someone if they are doing any kind of research at the moment	Ask someone if they have ever done a scientific experiment

Ask someone what time they make it (This means what time is it?)	Ask someone if an insect has ever done them any harm	Ask someone when the last time they made a complaint was
Ask someone if they know what kind of mistakes they make in English	Ask someone who makes the beds in their house	Ask someone if anyone has ever made them an interesting offer
Ask someone if they have ever made friends with someone abroad	Ask someone where they do their shopping	Ask someone if they have ever made a long journey
Ask someone if they think they are making progress in English and why	Ask someone if they have ever done more than 100km per hour in their car	Ask someone if they like making tea or coffee in the mornings
Ask someone what they do for a living	Ask someone if they have ever done a scientific experiment	Ask someone if they think phrasal verbs make sense
Ask someone if they like do-it-yourself	Ask someone how many times they do their nails per month	Ask someone if they have ever done business with someone
Ask someone if they have ever made a reservation in English	Ask someone if their neighbours make a lot of noise	Ask someone if they have made up their mind about anything recently
Ask someone if they think their family members make a mess at home	Ask someone if they know what a do-gooder is	Ask someone if anyone has done them a good turn today
Ask someone if they went to a do at the weekend (a do = a party/event)	Ask someone if they like their steak well done	Ask someone if they have ever done up their house (do up = redecorate)

MAKE AND DO GAME

MAKE AND DO CARDS

Ask someone how often they * the housework	Ask someone if they are * any kind of research at the moment	Ask someone if they have ever * a scientific experiment
Ask someone what time they * it	Ask someone if an insect has ever * them any harm	Ask someone when the last time they * a complaint was
Ask someone if they know what kind of mistakes they * in English	Ask someone who * the beds in their house	Ask someone if anyone has ever * them an interesting offer
Ask someone if they have ever * friends with someone abroad	Ask someone where they * their shopping	Ask someone if they have ever * a long journey
Ask someone if they think they are * progress in English and why	Ask someone -if they have ever * more than 100km per hour in their car	Ask someone if they like * tea or coffee in the mornings
Ask someone what they * for a living	Ask someone if they have ever * a scientific experiment	Ask someone if they think phrasal verbs * sense
Ask someone if they like *-it-yourself	Ask someone how many times they * their nails per month	Ask someone if they have ever * business with someone
Ask someone if they have ever * a reservation in English	Ask someone if their neighbours * a lot of noise	Ask someone if they have * up their mind about anything recently
Ask someone if they think their family members * a mess at home	Ask someone if they know what a *-gooder is	Ask someone if anyone has * them a good turn today
Ask someone if they went to a * at the weekend	Ask someone if they like their steak well *	Ask someone if they have ever * up their house

㉑ SHOP TIL' YOU DROP
A PARTIR DE B2

DÊ UM SET DAS CARTAS com os *role-plays* para cada par de alunos. Em diferentes setores de uma loja de departamentos, os pares irão viver os papéis de A — *customer* e B — *shop assistant*. Com suas respectivas cartas, os alunos deverão desempenhar suas personagens nas situações. Certifique-se que eles tenham a oportunidade de trocar as posições de cliente e assistente.

SHOP TIL' YOU DROP · ROLE PLAY CARDS

CLOTHING DEPARTMENT

A You would like to buy a special outfit for your daughter's wedding. You go to the clothing department. You find a nice suit and ask to try it on.

CLOTHING DEPARTMENT

B You work in the clothing department. A woman comes in to buy a special outfit for her daughter's wedding. She asks to try it on and you show her the dressing rooms. You think it looks too tight and the color doesn't suit her. Tell her this politely.

ELECTRICAL APPLIANCE DEPARTMENT

A You bought an iPod from the Electrical Appliance department 6 weeks ago. The iPod worked for a while, but has now stopped working. Unfortunately you don't have the receipt anymore. Complain to the shop assistant and ask for a refund.

ELECTRICAL APPLIANCE DEPARTMENT

B You work in the Electrical Appliance department. A man complains about an iPod he bought 6 weeks ago. He asks for a refund, but he doesn't have a receipt and there is only one month guarantee. Tell him he can't have a refund.

FURNITURE DEPARTMENT

A You would like to buy a bed. You went to the furniture department yesterday and found one that you liked and it was in the sale. When you go to buy it today, the shop assistant says that the sale ended yesterday and the price has gone up. Complain a lot and ask for the sale price.

FURNITURE DEPARTMENT

B You work in the furniture department. A woman comes in and says she saw a bed advertised in the sale yesterday and she wants to buy it. Unfortunately the sale finished yesterday and the price has gone up today. She complains and is making quite a scandal. First, try to sell it for the normal price. Then, say that you are going to talk to the manager and see if you can sell it for the sale price.

STATIONERY DEPARTMENT

A You go the stationery department. You are looking for a birthday card for your husband. You would like a humorous one, but not too goofy. Ask the shop assistant for some advice.

STATIONERY DEPARTMENT

B You work in the stationery department. A woman wants to buy a birthday card for her husband. She wants a humorous one, but not goofy. There are many cards. Give her some advice.

SPORTS DEPARTMENT

A You go to the Sports department. You would like to take up golf, but don't know what kind of equipment you need for the sport. Ask the shop assistant for some help.

SPORTS DEPARTMENT

B You work in the Sports department. A man asks your advice about golf equipment. He is new to the sport. Show him the golf balls, clubs, tees and shoes. Try to sell him the lot.

KITCHENWARE DEPARTMENT

A You go to the Kitchenware department. You would like to buy a tea set for a friend's Golden wedding anniversary. You would like something very specific — eight cups, plates and saucers, as you know your friend has a big family.

KITCHENWARE DEPARTMENT

B You work in the kitchenware department. A woman would like to buy a tea set of 8 cups, plates and saucers. Unfortunately, you don't have eight, but you have six. Try and convince her to take the set of six.

㉒ BRITISH FOOD
A PARTIR DE B2

CADA ALUNO RECEBE E LÊ uma cópia do texto *British food is awful — myth or reality*. Em grupos de quatro alunos, cada um deve concentrar-se em um parágrafo específico (A, B, C ou D) e relatar para o grupo aquilo de que se lembrar, sem consultar o texto.

BRITISH FOOD IS AWFUL – MYTH OR FACT?

A British food has a reputation all over the world for being tasteless, bland and greasy. Many foreigners who go to back to their countries after visiting Britain claim that they ate nothing but potatoes and overcooked vegetables while they were there. Is this reputation that Britain is the land of boring food really true?

B Let's look at two possible reasons behind this accusation. Firstly, during the second world war, many different kinds of foods were rationed, e.g. bananas, sugar and flour, which meant that many Europeans had to make do with what they had. Some of the older generation in Britain today can't stand seeing food wasted and cook just enough for their meal. Secondly, due to the cold weather, British people tend to eat more stodgy food consisting mainly of carbohydrates.

C However, nowadays British cuisine has really taken off with creative cooks such as Jamie Oliver and Nigella Lawson, who both have television programs. They tend to use fresh ingredients, as well as herbs and spices from different countries to produce delicious recipes. There is also a television program called *Ready, Steady, Cook* where 2 teams have to come up with a gourmet meal in a short time using limited ingredients.

D There is no doubt that immigrants in Britain have had an influence on British cooking, such as curry from India, Kebabs from Turkey and Chinese cooking. The British have learnt from other nations about different ingredients and are trying their hand at new recipes. All in all, I think that it is a myth to say that British food is awful nowadays as you can find delicious snacks and meals in many different restaurants and cafes all over Britain.

Em seguida, escreva as questões abaixo na lousa para serem discutidas em grupos.

> Do you know anyone who has been to the UK and has criticized the food?
>
> What did they say? Do you believe them?
>
> Has your country's food been influenced by other nations? In which way?
>
> Do you have any cooking programs on TV? Do you like them? Why?
>
> Have you ever eaten anything you really hated? Describe it.

(23) UNCOUNTABLE NOUNS
A PARTIR DE B2

LEIA EM VOZ ALTA AS PALAVRAS abaixo, pedindo aos alunos para escrevê-las.

Em seguida, coloque-as na lousa, checando com os alunos se os substantivos são *countable* ou *uncountable nouns*.

ANSWERS
COUNTABLE AND UNCOUNTABLE NOUNS

RICE	U	EQUIPMENT	U
MONEY	U	INFORMATION	U
PROBLEM	C	KNOWLEDGE	U
COMPUTER	C	MODEL	C
MILK	U	PROPOSAL	C
NEWS	U	THEORY	C
ADVICE	U	SLANG	U
LUGGAGE	U	TRAFFIC	U
RESEARCH	U	PROGRESS	U
RESEARCH PROJECT	C	MUSIC	U

Corte as cartas de *countable* e *uncountable nouns*, colocando-as viradas para baixo em uma mesa. Em grupos de três alunos, cada um deve escolher uma carta e terá 3 minutos para falar sobre o tópico ali contido. Durante a fala, os outros participantes não devem interromper, podendo, entretanto, fazer perguntas e desenvolver uma discussão sobre o assunto ao final. Verifique o uso de *countable* e *uncountable nouns*.

UNCOUNTABLE AND COUNTABLE NOUNS CARDS

Talk about how to make a favorite dish	Talk about something that has happened in the news recently	Talk about some advice you were given that you thought was very useful
Talk about some research you are working on or that you have done	Talk about how a piece of equipment works at home	Talk about your favorite music and a favorite song
Talk about something you have read recently which you found useful	Talk about the worst places for traffic in your city and offer some solutions	Talk about the progress you have made in English
Talk about a trip you went on recently	Talk about a problem you have had with your luggage	Talk about the advantages and disadvantages of the Internet
Talk about something you have recently learnt in your English course	Give the other students information about your hometown	Talk about a problem in your city and how you think it can be solved

㉔ COMPARATIVE AND SUPERLATIVE
A PARTIR DE B2

Distribua um set das cartas de *ASK* e *TELL* para grupos de três pessoas. Separe as cartas de ASK em um monte e as de TELL em outro. Cada grupo receberá também uma moeda.

Os participantes jogam a moeda: se der 'cara', uma carta de ASK é usada, se der 'coroa', a carta TELL é escolhida. Ao pegar a carta ASK, uma pergunta deve ser feita à pessoa à direita. Quando a carta for TELL, o jogador conta ao grupo o seu conteúdo. Verifique se os alunos estão usando o comparativo e o superlativo corretamente.

ASK CARDS

ASK SOMEONE	**ASK SOMEONE**
To compare himself/herself with his/her brother/sister's height	To compare two famous buildings
ASK SOMEONE	**ASK SOMEONE**
About the best film he/she has ever seen	About the best book he/she has ever read
ASK SOMEONE	**ASK SOMEONE**
About the furthest place he/she has travelled to	About the most interesting person he/she has met
ASK SOMEONE	**ASK SOMEONE**
About the funniest English lesson he/she has ever had	The most expensive product they have ever bought

ASK SOMEONE

To compare learning English to his/her own language

ASK SOMEONE

To compare living in a city to living in the countryside

ASK SOMEONE

To compare two animals he/she likes

ASK SOMEONE

About the worst vacation he/she has ever had

ASK SOMEONE

About the most peaceful place they have ever been to

ASK SOMEONE

To compare driving a car to riding a bike

ASK SOMEONE

To compare two different countries

ASK SOMEONE

To compare two different regions in his/her country

ASK SOMEONE

About the most difficult exam he/she has ever taken

ASK SOMEONE

About the most expensive meal he/she has ever had

ASK SOMEONE

About the cheapest bargain he/she has ever found

ASK SOMEONE

About his/her earliest memory of school

TELL CARDS

TELL EVERYONE

About the oldest member of your family

TELL EVERYONE

About the most boring film you have ever seen

TELL EVERYONE

About the longest time you have ever been awake

TELL EVERYONE

About the nicest pub/bar to go to in your town

TELL EVERYONE

About the biggest challenge you have ever had

TELL EVERYONE

About the happiest day of your life

TELL EVERYONE

About the most delicious dish in your country

TELL EVERYONE

About the most generous person you have ever met

TELL EVERYONE

About a famous person you admire and one you don't admire and why

TELL EVERYONE

About two different famous geographical features in your country

TELL EVERYONE

About the funniest joke you have ever heard

TELL EVERYONE

About the worst job you could ever imagine

TELL EVERYONE

About how the rich and the poor live in your country

TELL EVERYONE

About the worst habit you can imagine someone having

TELL EVERYONE

About the most exciting adventure you have ever had

TELL EVERYONE

About the oldest building in your town

TELL EVERYONE

About the most enjoyable party you have ever been to

TELL EVERYONE

About the best site you have ever seen on the internet

TELL EVERYONE

About the cleanest hotel you have ever been to

TELL EVERYONE

About the youngest member of your family

㉕ OPTICAL ILLUSIONS
A PARTIR DE B2

DÊ A CADA PAR DE ALUNOS uma cópia do *worksheet Optical Illusions*. As atividades devem ser realizadas seguindo as instruções do *worksheet*, focando nas palavras e expressões da tabela.

As respostas são:
1 *vase and two people;* **2** *a young woman and an old woman;*
3 *a jazz player and a young woman.*

OPTICAL ILLUSIONS

FONTE: WWW.BRAINGLE.COM/BRAINTEASERS

1 Look at these 3 images. Tell your partner what you can see. Use these words:

It might be a... › *It appears to be a...*

It could be a... › *Now, I've got it! It's a...*

It looks like it is a... › *Wow! That's amazing!*

I think/reckon it is a... › *God! I can't believe it!*

2 Play a game with your partner. Close your eyes and scribble something on a piece of paper. Your partner has to make a picture out of your scribble and describe what he/she is drawing.

3 Choose a picture/object from a magazine. Don't let your partner see it. Describe the picture/object, but do not say the word. Your partner has to guess what it is. Take it in turns to describe.

(26) MYSTERIOUS EVENTS
A PARTIR DE B2

DIVIDA OS ALUNOS EM PARES, sendo que o aluno A lê a história *The Mean Pumpkin* e o B, *Crop Circles* do *worksheet Mysterious Events*. Em seguida, cada um relata sua história. Ao final, proponha uma discussão com toda a classe sobre os eventos, dando as respostas e teorias (veja a seguir):

MYSTERIOUS EVENTS

A • THE MEAN PUMPKIN

A strange event took place around Halloween time at Cornell University, Ithaca, the USA. When students woke up on an autumn morning, they saw a hollowed-out pumpkin in the McGraw's tower spire. There was a light flickering inside the pumpkin's mouth and the object looked mean and fierce.

The McGraw Tower was built at the end of the nineteenth century and there are 161 stairs to the top of the tower. At night, access to the stairs is cut off so nobody could possibly get to the top from the inside. As the tower is so high, it would be very dangerous from the outside. So, how exactly did this pumpkin get there?

There was a lot of hoo-ha about the happening for weeks to follow and some students and staff had debates about how the pumpkin got there. Each department had its own theory. The more superstitious thought it had been the act of witches, others produced a scientific explanation for the strange phenomenon.

B · CROP CIRCLES

The British media first reported seeing crop circles in the early 1980s. By 1990 crop circles had exploded into the public mind as the new phenomenon changed from simple circular patterns into huge and complex, geometric formations. The crop circles are a worldwide phenomenon and each year new reports come from an ever-increasing number of countries. However, the main concentration of events is to be found in Southern England, many around ancient sites such as Stonehenge, Avebury and Silbury Hill (the largest manmade mound in Europe).

Although there are many theories as to their creation, none have been able to explain satisfactorily exactly how the circles are made. However, perhaps some of the most persuasive evidence comes in the form of video taped footage showing small bright balls of white light in and around the crop circles. Other theories include the possibilities that hoaxers are responsible for the circles or even UFOs.

FONTES: WWW.CORNELL.EDU · WWW.CROPCIRCLECONNECTOR.COM

1 The story of the pumpkin in McGraw Tower is true, but later they found out that pranksters had climbed to the top of the tower with ropes and placed the pumpkin there.

2 Although a lot of research has been done on crop circles, no one really knows how they appear. The most probable theory is some kind of residual electro-magnetic field being left in the location of crop circles as batteries are drained very quickly in a crop circle.

(27) INTRUDERS SAY SORRY
A PARTIR DE B2

Esta atividade é dividida em três partes. Primeiramente, introduza o título da história a ser lida — *Intruders say sorry* — discutindo possíveis desenvolvimentos.

Em seguida, cada aluno recebe uma cópia da história e a preenche com as palavras propostas. Ao checar as respostas, as mesmas devem ser colocadas na lousa.

Para finalizar, em pares, um aluno começa a recontar a história usando a primeira palavra da lousa. O outro aluno continua, fazendo uso da segunda palavra e assim por diante até que toda a lista seja concluída.

RESPOSTAS
INTRUDERS SAY SORRY

1 *knife*	**6** *police*	**11** *was assaulted*
2 *wooden club*	**7** *Forensic teams*	**12** *raise the alarm*
3 *breaking into*	**8** *forced*	**13** *attack*
4 *injuries*	**9** *intruders*	
5 *drugs*	**10** *distressed*	

INTRUDERS SAY SORRY
Fill in the gaps with the words from the box

INTRUDERS	ATTACK	FORCED
KNIFE	BREAKING INTO	DRUGS
RAISE THE ALARM	INJURIES	WAS ASSAULTED
WOODEN CLUB	FORENSIC TEAMS	
DISTRESSED	POLICE	

INTRUDERS AT WRONG HOUSE SAY SORRY

A young mother was recovering yesterday after two men armed with a _____ and a _____ broke into her bedroom at 2am, only to apologise and say that they had targeted the wrong house.

The pair then left quietly before _____ the woman's neighbors' and attacking a young man who was left with head _____.

An underworld feud or _____ quarrel are among motives being examined for the bizarre incident by South Yorkshire _____, who cordoned off the scene of the attack at Swinton, south Yorkshire yesterday. _____ are checking both properties while the woman, who has two small children, recovers from severe shock.

A spokesman for the police said that the men, wearing high visibility work vests _____ the back door to her house at 2am on Monday, and ran upstairs to the bedroom. One had the knife and the other the crude club made from a wooden plank.

"But it soon became obvious that the _____ had got the wrong address and they left, apologizing," said the spokesman. "No threats were made, although the woman was left in a _____ state."

The men then went next door in Station Street, close to the center of the small town near Rotherham, which is the hub of the remaining commercial waterway barge fleets in South Yorkshire. The spokesman said: "Inside the premises a 23-year old male _____ and required hospital treatment."

Other occupants fled unscathed to _____ and the attackers left hastily. Both were white and in their 20s and made no attempt to be inconspicuous in their reflective work vests. The woman was said to have been "absolutely terrified" at the time of the _____ but is making a good recovery.

FONTE: WAINWRIGHT, M. *INTRUDERS AT WRONG HOUSE SAY SORRY*, GUARDIAN, 29/12/04, P. 7

(28) **DEPENDENT PREPOSITIONS**
A PARTIR DE B2

EM PARES, OS ALUNOS TENTAM descobrir as habilidades do parceiro por meio das seguintes perguntas: *What are you good at? What are you bad at?*

Cada aluno receberá e irá completar as frases do *work-sheet Dependent Prepositions*. Verifique as respostas e coloque as preposições na lousa. Em pares, os alunos devem fazer perguntas e dar as respostas usando as frases com as devidas preposições.

Por exemplo:
What kind of leisure activity are you interested in?
I am interested in swimming. I go every week. It's good because it relaxes me...

RESPOSTAS
DEPENDENT PREPOSITIONS

I am very interested IN

I am keen ON

I was always very good AT

I am responsible FOR

I have strong opinions ABOUT

I have great admiration FOR because

The last time I complimented (somebody) ON (something) was when

I am excited ABOUT (something next week)

I am afraid OF (animal)

My nationality is different FROM (another nationality) because

The smell of (smell) always reminds me OF

I am so tired OF (something you do every day)

DEPENDENT PREPOSITIONS

Complete the sentences using the correct preposition

I am very interested _____ (leisure activity)

I am keen _____ (food/drink)

I was always very good _____ (school subject)

I am responsible _____ (job)

I have strong opinions _____ (something in the news)

I have great admiration _____ (a person) because

The last time I complimented (somebody) _____ (something) was when

I am excited _____ (something next week)

I am afraid _____ (animal)

My nationality is different _____ (another nationality) because

The smell of (smell) always reminds me _____

I am so tired _____ (something you do every day)

㉙ CONTROVERSIAL TOPICS
A PARTIR DE C1

DÊ A CADA ALUNO UMA CÓPIA das expressões *For and Against*.
Cheque o entendimento.

Corte os tópicos da planilha *Controversial Topics*, distri-
buindo-os em montes para grupos de três pessoas.

Os tópicos devem ser posicionados em uma mesa vira-
dos para baixo. Cada aluno pega seu tópico, o lê em voz alta
e elabora sua opinião por dois minutos. Os outros participantes se juntam à discussão fazendo uso das expressões da
tabela ao final deste período. O mesmo procedimento deve
ser adotado para todos do grupo.

FOR AND AGAINST EXPRESSIONS

FOR	AGAINST
More diplomatic	**More diplomatic**
Yeah, I'd go along with you on that one.	Ok, I get your point, but...
Yeah, exactly my thoughts too.	But if you were in my position, wouldn't you think the same?
Wow, really! I couldn't agree more.	Everyone has got a point of view, but I still think...
I feel exactly the same as you.	
Yeah, I didn't think of it like that, but you're right.	**Less diplomatic**
Do you think so...?	Come on!
Yeah, I suppose you've got a point there.	I can't believe you're saying that!
	That is nonsense/rubbish!
	You've got to be joking!

CONTROVERSIAL TOPICS

All couples should live together before getting married	Men and women are practically equal nowadays
Experiments carried out on animals should be banned	Prejudice against foreigners in my country has improved over the last ten years
Customer service in huge companies and big supermarkets should be improved	Video games and violent films should be banned for our children's sake
The government should pay for all education	Reality shows are like a human zoo and I have had enough of watching them
The Internet should be made available to everyone and the government should pay for it	The prison system in my country needs improving

㉚ ANY REGRETS, Mr. PRESIDENT?
A PARTIR DE C1

CORTE AS TRÊS POSIÇÕES DA PLANILHA *Any Regrets, Mr. President?* e divida a classe em três grupos:

Grupo 1 › *opposition to the President*
Grupo 2 › *supporters of the President*
Grupo 3 › *President and First Lady (somente duas pessoas)*

Em seus grupos, os alunos têm 15 minutos para discutirem suas posições que devem ser defendidas em uma reunião geral.

O grupo 3 deve se posicionar na frente da classe e o professor é responsável pela condução da reunião. O grupo 1 expõem suas ideias e o grupo 3 se defende. Em seguida, o grupo 2 expressa suas opiniões e o professor media a discussão e o tempo.

ANY REGRETS, MR. PRESIDENT?

OPPOSITION TO THE PRESIDENT

Imagine that the President of your country for the last 4 years was not re-elected again. You do not support his party and did not re-elect him. Make a list with your partner of all the things you think he should not have done in his term in office. Think about health, education, agriculture, distribution of wealth, privatization, culture and the arts, unemployment, crime, foreign affairs, the economy, a scandal involving the President and anything else you wish to remember. Afterwards, present what you have discussed at a general meeting.

SUPPORTERS OF THE PRESIDENT

Imagine that the President of your country for the last 4 years was not re-elected again. You supported his party and are sad that he was not re-elected. Make a list with your partner of all the things you wish he had done better in his term in office. Think about health, education, agriculture, distribution of wealth, privatization, culture and the arts, unemployment, crime, foreign affairs, the economy, a scandal involving the President and anything else you wish to remember. Afterwards present what you have discussed at a general meeting.

PRESIDENT AND FIRST LADY

You are the President and the First Lady. The President was in office for 4 years, but was not re-elected again. You are going to take part in a general meeting where there is a group of supporters and a group from the opposition. They are going to tell you what you shouldn't have done and what you could have done better. The topics they are discussing are: health, education, agriculture, distribution of wealth, privatization, culture and the arts, unemployment, crime, foreign affairs, the economy, a scandal involving you and anything else they wish to remember. You must be ready to defend yourselves, as you would not like to lose face in case of being re-elected in the future. Be assertive!

㉛ **PUBS**
A PARTIR DE C1

DIVIDA OS ALUNOS EM DOIS GRUPOS — A e B. Dê a cada aluno do grupo A as questões do *Pubs* e a cada aluno do grupo B o texto da *Activity 1*. O grupo A discute as perguntas e tenta predizer as respostas. O grupo B checa o entendimento do texto. Organize pares com um aluno A e um B. O A faz as perguntas ao B o qual, por sua vez, as responde de acordo com o texto. O mesmo procedimento deve ser feito com a *Activity 2*, invertendo-se os papéis.

ACTIVITY 1

STUDENT A
1 What is a pub?
2 How old do you have to be to drink in a pub in the UK?
3 Are children allowed in pubs?
4 What time do pubs open and close in the UK?
5 What does it mean when the landlord/lady shouts "last orders"?

ACTIVITY 2

STUDENT B
1 Do you think you order drinks and food at the bar or at the table in a pub?
2 When do you pay for your drink?
3 Should you tip the barman/woman?
4 Can you smoke in a pub?
5 Can you play games in pubs?

ACTIVITY 1

STUDENT B

WHAT IS A PUB?

A pub (public house) is a place where alcoholic drinks can be bought and drunk and where food is often available.

DRINKING AGE IN THE UNITED KINGDOM

You can buy an alcoholic drink in the UK if you're over the age of 18. One word of advice — if you look young, you may be asked for identification.

FAMILIES

Some pubs allow families in for meals and some don't. Some even have areas where children can play, but they still require parents to supervise their offspring.

OPENING AND CLOSING TIMES

A law was recently passed for pubs to stay open 24 hours. It is up to each individual Landlord to apply for opening hours to suit his/her own establishment, so each pub can be different.

LAST ORDERS

Landlords/Landladies usually call "last orders" ten minutes before closing time and you can buy a drink up to closing time. "Last orders" is often indicated by ringing a bell and calling "last orders at the bar". When time is called, that's it — you can't buy booze to take home at this point.

ACTIVITY 2

STUDENT A

ORDERING DRINKS AND FOOD

Generally you order your drink from the bar and take it to where your friends are sitting/standing. You often order food from the bar too, although food will usually be brought to you after ordering. When you go to the bar to order a drink and if there's a group with you, don't all go together, there won't be room. One or two of you should go and order the drinks and bring them back.

PAYING FOR DRINKS

You usually pay for the drink when you order. The normal thing to do is to buy a round for everyone in your group. Afterwards someone will offer to buy the next round and so on.

TIPPING

If you feel someone in the pub has provided exceptional service you can offer to buy him or her a drink. Sometimes, he or she will actually take the drink (and drink it with you).

SMOKING

The whole of the United Kingdom became subject to a ban on smoking in enclosed public places in 2007.

GAMES

In some pubs you can play games such as darts, snooker, and shove ha' penny. You can also gamble on slot machines. Sometimes pubs organize general knowledge quizzes.

FONTE: WWW.FANCYAPINT.COM

㉜ COMMON ERRORS
A PARTIR DE C1

Em pares, os alunos recebem a planilha *Common Errors* e marcam as palavras corretas em cada frase. Confira as respostas abaixo.

Corte as cartas e dê um set para cada dupla, com as palavras viradas para baixo em uma mesa. Ao pegar uma carta, o aluno A deve formular uma frase com aquela palavra. O aluno B checa o uso na frase. Em seguida, os papeis se invertem.

RESPOSTAS

1 cook	**8** experiment	**15** take
2 stole	**9** story	**16** nice
3 remind	**10** library borrow	**17** teaching
4 hear	**11** relatives	**18** got
5 looks	**12** prescription	**19** physician
6 arguing	**13** current actually	**20** sensitive
7 grey dyed	**14** exhibition	

COMMON ERRORS · CARDS

Cook	Experience	Actual	Physician
Cooker	Experiment	Current	Sensible
Steal	History	Actually	Sensitive
Rob	Story	Presently	Borrow
Remember	Library	Nice	Lend
Remind	Bookshop	Sympathetic	Physicist
Hear	Parents	Teach	Prescription
Listen to	Relatives	Learn	Argue
Discuss	Recipe	Win	Dye

COMMON ERRORS

1 The cook/cooker in this restaurant must be excellent. The food is superb.

2 Somebody stole/robbed my wallet. It was in my back pocket 10 minutes ago.

3 Can you remind/remember me to go to the bank. I have to get some money out the ATM.

4 Did you listen to/hear the news about that terrible tragedy? Those poor people!

5 She looks/looks like nice. I think I'm going to offer her a drink.

6 My neighbors are always discussing/arguing. It must be terrible for the kids.

7 My Granny has got white/grey hair. She painted/dyed it for many years, but now she's left it natural.

8 My scientific experiment/experience was a success. My supervisor was really pleased.

9 I used to love that history/story of Little Red Riding Hood. My Mum used to tell it to me.

10 I always go to the library/bookshop to lend/borrow a book for the weekend.

11 I have many relatives/parents all over the country, but I hardly ever see them.

12 The doctor gave me a recipe/prescription for some medicine.

13 My actual/current job is great. It is the best job I've ever had actually/presently.

14 The exhibition/exposition of Monet's famous masterpieces was absolutely amazing.

15 I have to take/pass an exam on Friday. I should get the results in 2 weeks' time.

16 My new teacher is so sympathetic/nice. In the first lesson she made such a good impression.

17 I have been teaching/learning foreign students for 6 years. It is such a rewarding job.

18 I won/got a fantastic present from my parents for Christmas. It was a brand new car!

19 I am a physicist/physician. My patients come to my surgery to be diagnosed.

20 My mum is so sensible/sensitive. She always cries when we go to the cinema.

A AUTORA

Jane Godwin Coury nasceu no Reino Unido e vem trabalhando como professora de inglês e treinadora de professores no Brasil desde 1994. Ela também já trabalhou no Reino Unido, na França e nos Estados Unidos como professora de inglês. Ela é examinadora dos exames Cambridge e possui mestrado em Linguística Aplicada e TESOL da Universidade de Leicester no Reino Unido. Jane é sócia (com outras três profissionais) da escola de inglês THE FOUR em São Carlos, SP, Brasil.

AGRADECIMENTOS

Gostaria de agradecer a minha família tanto no Brasil quanto no Reino Unido por seu amor e apoio, em particular a Denis, Isabella, Julia e meus pais, por sua disponibilidade infinda. Gostaria também de agradecer minhas três sócias, Maj-Lis Strunk Costa, Silvana Vieira Dibo e Solange Moras por seu entusiasmo e apoio na criação da nossa escola, THE FOUR. Minha gratidão também se estende a Anna Szabó e Jane Revell que me deram infinitas oportunidades para crescer como profissional. Um agradecimento especial a Silvana Vieira Dibo, Beverly Young e Denis Coury pela revisão do texto e Isabella e Julia pela inestimável ajuda com a tradução. Meus agradecimentos são também extensivos à Disal pela publicação deste livro.

In loving memory of Gladys Butcher.

MATERIAL DE APOIO

FACTFILES

CANADA FACTFILE

POPULATION: approximately 34 million

CAPITAL: Ottawa

CURRENCY: 1 Canadian dollar (Can$) = 100 cents

TYPICAL FOOD: salmon, cod cakes, maple syrup desserts

NATIONAL SPORTS: ice hockey, skiing

TOURIST SIGHTS: Niagra falls, Banff, Montreal, Vancouver

USA FACTFILE

POPULATION: approximately 313 million

CAPITAL: Washington DC

CURRENCY: 1 dollar ($) = 100 cents

TYPICAL FOOD: Hamburgers and French fries, hot dogs, pancakes, baked potatoes, apple pie

NATIONAL SPORTS: American football, baseball, basketball

TOURIST SIGHTS: Niagra falls, Hollywood, Rocky mountains, The Great lakes, New York

FACTFILES

ENGLAND FACTFILE

POPULATION: approximately 51 million

CAPITAL: London

CURRENCY: 1 pound (£) = 100 pennies

TYPICAL FOOD: fish and chips, roast beef, steak and kidney pie, ploughman's lunch, curry

NATIONAL SPORTS: football, rugby, cricket, golf, horse riding

TOURIST SIGHTS: London, Bath, Oxford, Cambridge.

AUSTRALIA FACTFILE

POPULATION: approximately 22 million

CAPITAL: Canberra

CURRENCY: 1 Australian dollar (\$AUS) = 100 cents

TYPICAL FOOD: meat pie, barbecues, kangaroo tail soup

NATIONAL SPORTS: rugby, basketball, surfing

TOURIST SIGHTS: The Great Barrier Reef, Sydney, Ayers Rock

SMALL TALK GAME

Board 1

START
- Ask what the main national sports are in his/her country
- Ask what kind of food is typical from his/her country
- Ask what the capital of his/her country is
- Ask about his/her family
- Free question
- Ask him/her to describe his/her job
- Ask what the weather is like in his/her country
- Ask how he/she spends his/her weekends

Board 2

START
- Ask where he/she is from
- Ask what the main tourist sights are in his/her country
- Ask if he/she had any problems getting here
- Ask what the hotel is like
- Free question
- Ask what the currency is from his/her country
- Ask which countries he/she has visited
- Ask about the place where he/she was brought up

Board 3

START
- Ask what typical food there is in his/her country
- Free question
- Ask what his/her interests are
- Ask what kind of music he/she likes
- Ask what a tourist can do in his/her country
- Ask if he/she has any brothers or sisters
- Ask what the most common sports are in his/her country
- Ask what the capital city is like in his/her country

Board 4

START
- Ask what the national dish in his/her country is
- Ask what his/her job entails
- Ask what kind of films he/she likes
- Free question
- Ask what the population is of his/her country
- Ask what the currency of his/her country is
- Ask what tourist sights there are in his/her country
- Ask what he/she thinks of computers

JOB INTERVIEW • ROLEPLAY A AND B

ROLE PLAY A • EMPLOYER

You should ask the candidate the following questions and invent 4 more questions. Remember you need someone who has at least 3 years of work experience in a reputable company. After you have finished asking questions, ask him/her if he/she has any doubts.

What is your full name?
Where are you from?
Which qualifications do you have?
Tell me what skills you learnt at university.
What work experience do you have?
Tell me your strong points and weak points of working in a group at work.
Why do you want this job?
What hobbies do you have which make you feel relaxed?
What is your biggest achievement in life?

ROLEPLAY B • CANDIDATE

Your employer is going to interview you. You have a university degree in Business Administration and you were an Honors student. After university, you travelled around the world for 6 months. Then you got a job in a company which is not well known. After 2 years you got fired because you were not good at working in groups. You really want this job, so try to convince the employer you are the right person. You should ask him/her any questions at the end.

ALTERNATIVE LIFESTYLES STUDENT A

STUDENT A

HOUSEBOAT DWELLER

BACKGROUND

My name is John, I am single and I just turned 45. I am tall and have dark curly brown hair and blue eyes. I am from the southwest of England. I work as a cook in a country pub from 11am to 3pm and sometimes 6pm to 10pm.

MY ALTERNATIVE LIFE

I have made my home on a narrow boat on a canal. Some people may find it strange living on the water, but I love it. It is very peaceful and you can wake up in the morning listening to the birds singing outside. There is no problem in falling asleep as the boat is always swaying to and fro. I moor my boat near a main town, where I can get all my groceries and where there are facilities, such as a sports centre, a cinema and a theatre. My friends and relatives come to stay with me sometimes at weekends and we enjoy sitting on the bank fishing together. There is a big community of people living on houseboats near me, so you can always count on a friend for anything you need.

REASONS

I chose this lifestyle for two main reasons. First of all, because house prices in the UK are very expensive and I couldn't afford to buy a house. Secondly I wanted to leave the big city life and live as close to nature as possible.

STUDENT B
BACKPACKER

BACKGROUND

I am called Susan and I am 26 years old. I am single and I graduated from university when I was 22 years old. I am quite short and slim. I have blonde hair and green eyes. I have a degree in Modern Languages — French and Spanish. After university, I worked on the Eurostar train, which goes through the channel tunnel connecting the UK to France. I was a waitress and had to speak both French and English.

MY ALTERNATIVE LIFE

When I was 24 years old, I left my job at Eurostar and decided to see more of the world. I bought a backpack, a pair of good sneakers, some casual clothes and a round-the-world ticket. First of all, I went to the USA and ended up working as a housekeeper in a hotel in California. After that I caught a plane to South America and travelled around Brazil, Argentina and Chile. Then I went on to South Africa and worked in a McDonalds for 6 months in Johannesburg. I am currently travelling around Africa and plan to go to Asia afterwards.

REASONS

I made up my mind to set off on a huge journey like this because I was quite bored with life in the UK and wanted to experience different cultures and see how people live. It is completely different from being a tourist.

REGULAR VERBS IN THE PAST

Put these verbs into the different columns according to their sound and looking at the rules below

	/d/	/t/	/id/
asked			
believed			
called			
closed			
developed			
enjoyed			
hated			
kissed			
liked			
loved			
opened			
painted			
showed			
talked			
watched			
washed			
worked			

Generally, if a word in its present form ends in:

e, n, y, l, w	it has the /d/ sound
k, ss, sh, ch, p	it has the /t/ sound
t, te, d	it has the /id/ sound

LIFE CYCLE • USEFUL VOCABULARY

USEFUL VOCABULARY

Teller	Listener
Did I tell you about the time when...?	No, tell me about it
You'll never guess what!	Really?
The funniest experience I've ever had was...	I can't believe it! You did what?
Then/After that....	Wow! That's amazing!
The best/worst part was...	It sounds really great/bad
It was such a good laugh	Yeah, then what happened?
It was awful!	It must have been hilarious!
What was really strange/ weird was...	God! What a nightmare!
Finally....	So, what did you do?
	What happened in the end?

USEFUL VOCABULARY

Teller	Listener
Did I tell you about the time when...?	No, tell me about it
You'll never guess what!	Really?
The funniest experience I've ever had was...	I can't believe it! You did what?
Then/After that....	Wow! That's amazing!
The best/worst part was...	It sounds really great/bad
It was such a good laugh	Yeah, then what happened?
It was awful!	It must have been hilarious!
What was really strange/ weird was...	God! What a nightmare!
Finally....	So, what did you do?
	What happened in the end?

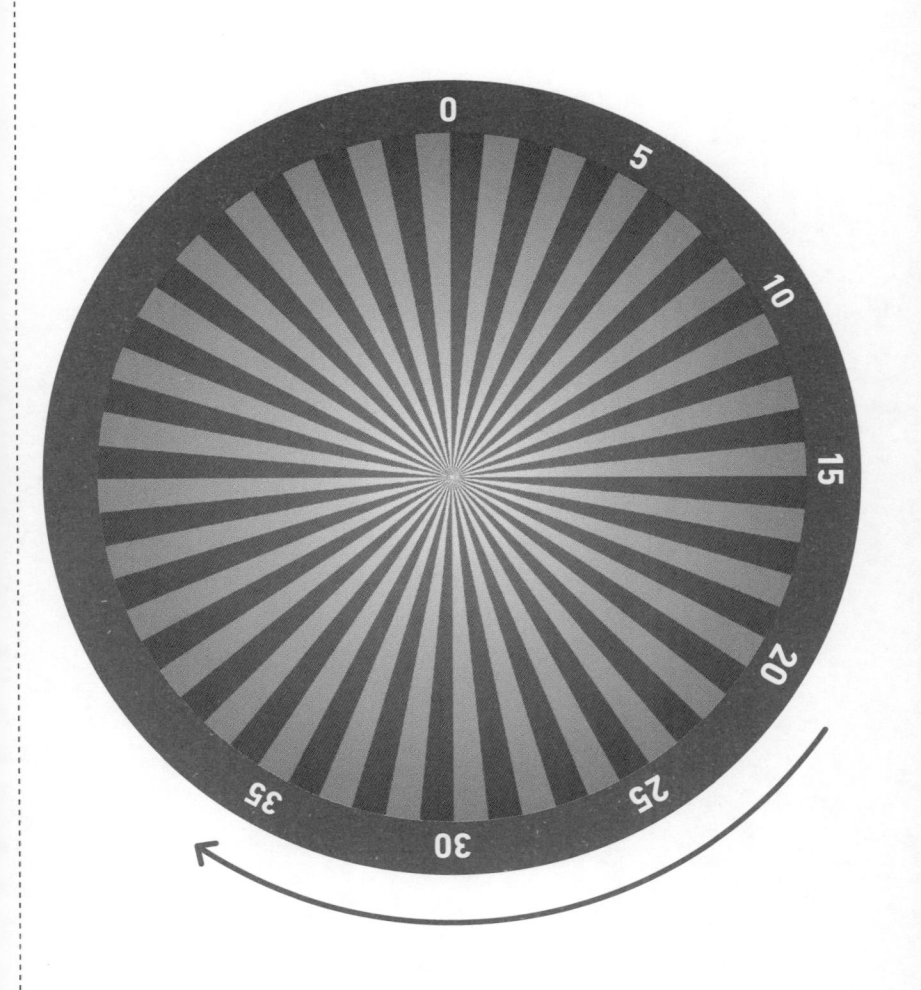

MILESTONES IN MY EDUCATION/CAREER

My earliest memory of school was...

When I was at elementary school I remember + ing...

When I went to high school, I felt...

I first started getting interested in ... when I was ... years old.

I spent ... years studying for my university entrance exam.

I studied all kinds of subjects including...

I got into university when I was ... years old

I got/I am studying for a degree in (*subject*)...

I did/I am doing work experience at (*place*)...

Our graduation ball was amazing/a disaster/ interesting because...

My happiest memory of university was...

Afterwards, I did a Master's/PhD in...

I got a job at (*the place*) in (*the year*).

I had to do a lot of interviews and I was short listed to 6 candidates.

Luckily, I got a job as a (*profession*)

Looking back, I think...

IRREGULAR VERBS

VERB	PAST SIMPLE
begin	
break	
buy	
catch	
choose	
drink	
eat	
fly	
forget	
hear	
know	
leave	
meet	
pay	
read	
say	
speak	
tell	
think	
understand	

PEOPLE DESCRIPTION · PHYSICAL APPEARANCE

He/She has got	light	blonde	
	dark	brown	
	jet	black	HAIR
	fiery	red	
		grey	

He/She has got	short		
	long		
	straight		HAIR
	curly		
	wavy		

He/She has got	piercing	blue	
	emerald	green	EYES
	dark	brown	
	hazel	coloured	

He/She is	white/black
	quite tall/short
	lanky
	plump
	slim
	skinny
	barefoot

He/She has got	striking features
	high cheek bones
	a pale/dark/olive complexion

He/She looks like	a model
	an American/a Brazilian
	a nice person
	he/she is in her twenties
	a talkative person
	a shy person

He/She looks	friendly/unfriendly
	healthy/fit
	kind
	well dressed/scruffy
	old/young
	stressed-out
	strikingly handsome (man)
	extremely beautiful (woman)

PEOPLE DESCRIPTION · CLOTHES

She is wearing	a blouse
	a top
	a T-shirt
	a skirt
	a dress
	a pair of trousers/jeans
	a jumper/sweater
	a coat/jacket
	a pair of tights/socks
	a bra
	a bikini
	a swimsuit
He is wearing	a shirt
	a T-shirt
	a pair of trousers/jeans
	a jumper/sweater
	a suit
	a tie
	a coat/jacket
	a pair of Boxer shorts
	a pair of socks
	a pair of pyjamas

FOOTWEAR

He/She is wearing a pair of shoes	sneakers
	sandals
	high heeled shoes
	flip flops
	slippers

ACCESSORIES

He/She is wearing	a pair of glasses
	a hat/cap
	a scarf
	a pair of gloves

ADJECTIVES

striped/checked/spotted/flowery/dark brown/light green/lovely/
cool/horrible/disgusting.

SOAP OPERA

For each picture fill in the following information:

Name	
Age	
Marital status	
Profession	
Interests	

Name	
Age	
Interests	

Name	
Age	
Marital status	
Profession	
Interests	

Name	
Age	
Marital status	
Profession	
Interests	

WHAT WOULD YOU DO?

1 *Imagine you are walking down the road, when you see someone being pick-pocketed. What would you do?*

2 *You are in a foreign country and your host serves a strange looking dish. When you ask what it is, he says it is pig's eyes — a delicacy. What would you do?*

3 *You go to a conference and your power point presentation does not work. What would you do?*

4 *You see your friend's husband having a romantic dinner with a woman in a restaurant, who is not his wife. What would you do?*

5 *You go to a beach with your friend and when you arrive you find out it is a nudist beach. What would you do?*

6 *You receive an invitation through the post to take part in a reality show on TV. What would you do?*

7 *You have invited your parents-in-law for dinner and in the middle of the meal, a cockroach crawls across the table. What would you do?*

8 *You dye your hair black for a fancy dress party. When you wash it the next day, your hair goes green! What would you do?*

9 *A native speaker tells a joke in English and you don't get it. What would you do?*

10 *You find £100 in the bathroom at an airport. What would you do?*

11 *You buy something in a shop and notice that the cashier has shortchanged you for a product. What would you do?*

12 *You share a house with 3 other people. You open the fridge and it stinks of a French cheese that your friend bought on vacation. What would you do?*

13 *Your colleague has terrible B.O. (body odour) and it is bothering you. What would you do?*

14 *You notice that your colleague is wearing one red sock and one blue one. What would you do?*

15 *In a meeting your boss tells everyone some information that you know is incorrect. What would you do?*

16 *You are on holiday in a foreign country and you park in a no parking zone. You get a parking ticket. What would you do?*

17 *Your friend wins a free makeover at a department store. When you see her, you think she looks awful. What would you do?*

18 *You borrow a book from your English teacher and on the way home it gets sopping wet. What would you do?*

19 *You have invited a foreigner to your home for a meal. At the end of the meal, he burps. What would you do?*

20 *You buy a car from a second hand dealer who assures you the air conditioning is working. After you have bought it, you find out there is no air conditioning! What would you do?*

PROFILE • THE CRITIC

Nothing you do is good enough. This person's comments always provoke you or initiate competition. Typical things he/she says are *'the turkey is delicious but you have been so overworked that I think you left it too long in the oven'* or *Christmas at so and so's house was much better last year. She is a great hostess'* and so on.

HOW TO DEAL WITH THIS PERSON

The best way is to let him/her feel important. For example, in the case of the turkey, say that your turkey is not as good as his/hers and ask for their advice to improve the recipe. Asking for co-operation is always a good way of avoiding competition. People who are like this, need to be recognized. They need approval from people for things they do.

PROFILE • THE DRUNK

The more they drink, the more intense they get. They start hugging people, crying and giggling. Sometimes they even want to tell rude jokes that don't go down very well and no one finds them funny.

HOW TO DEAL WITH THIS PERSON

Keep cool. If you get offended by anything they say, the party could end up in a fight. If you are the hostess/host and notice that this person is annoying the other guests, discretely lead them away and take them somewhere else. Don't think about hiding the booze as this could cause the person to get angry. If you don't want drunk people at your party, don't serve alcohol.

PROFILE • THE HYPOCHONDRIAC

This person goes on and on about their illnesses and they talk in detail about the medicine they are taking. A conversation with them goes something like this *'today I woke up with a terrible pain in my side. Do you think it is serious? They say that this is a symptom of bird flu. Yesterday I had a backache and took some medicine and I think my liver has been affected now. I took something else for my liver and then I almost died of stomachache. Do you think I am going to get bird flu?'*

HOW TO DEAL WITH THIS PERSON

Be patient. This kind of person is normally an attention seeker. If the conversation gets too unbearable say "*now tell me something good that's happening in your life.*" Try to get them to talk about positive things. Try not to be sucked into their world and start saying "*Oh me too*" as this may lead to a competition of who is the worst victim!

PROFILE • THE LAZY GUY

He/She always arrives late and empty handed. Other people's houses are an extension of their own, which means they feel free to meddle with your things, wee in your bathroom with the door open or lie down on the sofa with their shoes on. They will probably ask for more tea or cake while lounging on the sofa and they never offer to clean up.

HOW TO DEAL WITH THIS PERSON

Say "*Please feel free to get a piece of cake yourself. It's in the kitchen.*" By doing this you won't be at their beck and call all the time. If you are upset about them meddling with your things, close the door of the room where you want privacy. Hide things you don't want visitors to touch or see. If you want them to help, ask. For example you could say "Could you please put your dirty cup in the kitchen and when they are in the kitchen, hand them a tea towel and ask them to dry up."

PROFILE • THE GOSSIPER

They know sordid details about everyone's lives and don't miss a chance to gossip about someone. They have an intense morbid pleasure in exposing people's secrets.

HOW TO DEAL WITH THIS PERSON

Try not to listen to gossip and discretely leave. If there is no way out, listen quietly without making comments which can be used against you. Do not repeat anything you heard as this only spreads gossip. If it involves anyone who is there, call the person over to take part in the conversation and find out if it is true.

ADOPTING A CHILD

A truck driver was in a service station and was just about to get into his truck when he heard a baby crying. He looked under his truck and saw a one-week old baby boy screaming right in front of his wheel. He picked the baby up and took him to the authorities. Now the baby is up for adoption and the authorities are looking for the ideal parents.

Mark each item of the list of criteria below on a scale of 1 (very important) to 5 (not important at all). Then, get into groups of 3 and discuss each point. Use the agreeing and disagreeing phrases in your discussion.

CRITERIA

The ideal parents should:

❑ be under 30 yrs old
❑ be of the same racial group as the child
❑ be of the same religious group as each other
❑ be a married couple
❑ be a heterosexual couple
❑ both have jobs
❑ have other children in the family
❑ not be living in poverty
❑ have some professional experience of dealing with children, i.e. as teachers or nurses

THE BEATLES QUIZ

1 Where were the Beatles from?
a London
b Liverpool
c New York

2 What was the name of John Lennon´s first group?
a The Beat up
b The Beetles
c The Quarrymen

3 Who thought of the name The Beatles?
a John Lennon
b Paul McCartney
c George Harrison

4 Which song was The Beatles first UK hit?
a Lucy in the Sky with Diamonds
b Love me Do
c Yesterday

5 Which country did The Beatles go to in 1968 to learn about meditation?
a India
b Tibet
c The USA

6 When did the Beatles split up?
a 1969
b 1970
c 1971

7 How did John Lennon die?
a He died of cancer
b He was shot
c He died in a car accident

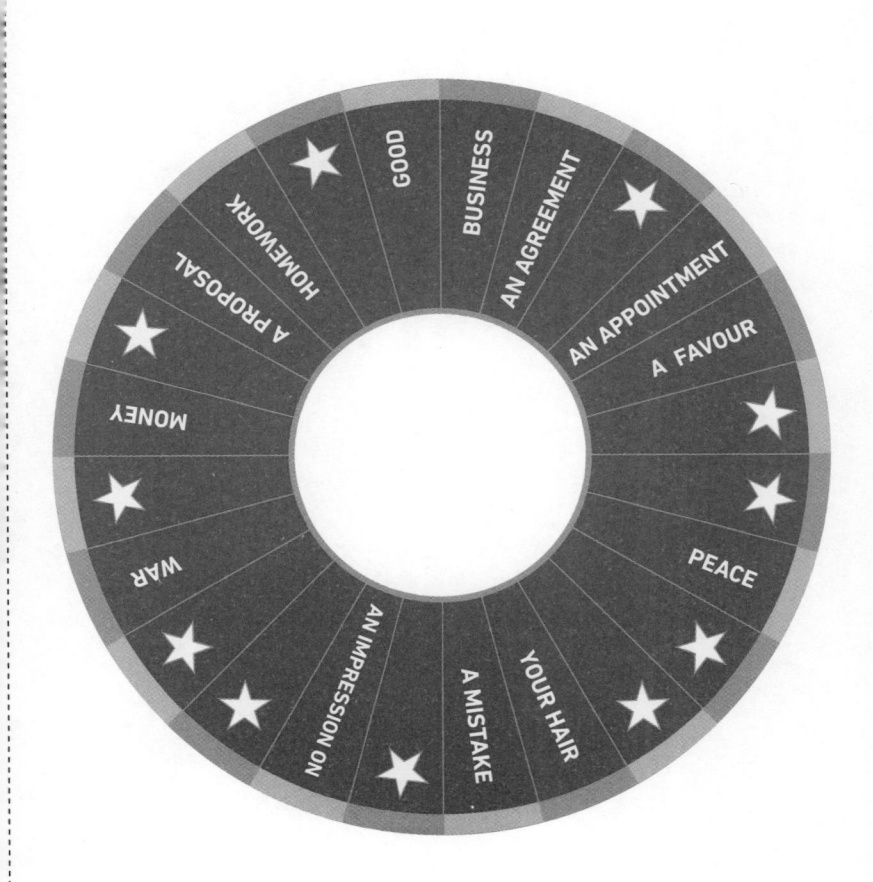

MAKE AND DO CARDS

Ask someone how often they * the housework	Ask someone if they are * any kind of research at the moment	Ask someone if they have ever * a scientific experiment
Ask someone what time they * it	Ask someone if an insect has ever * them any harm	Ask someone when the last time they * a complaint was
Ask someone if they know what kind of mistakes they * in English	Ask someone who * the beds in their house	Ask someone if anyone has ever * them an interesting offer
Ask someone if they have ever * friends with someone abroad	Ask someone where they * their shopping	Ask someone if they have ever * a long journey
Ask someone if they think they are * progress in English and why	Ask someone -if they have ever * more than 100km per hour in their car	Ask someone if they like * tea or coffee in the mornings
Ask someone what they * for a living	Ask someone if they have ever * a scientific experiment	Ask someone if they think phrasal verbs * sense
Ask someone if they like *-it-yourself	Ask someone how many times they * their nails per month	Ask someone if they have ever * business with someone
Ask someone if they have ever * a reservation in English	Ask someone if their neighbours * a lot of noise	Ask someone if they have * up their mind about anything recently
Ask someone if they think their family members * a mess at home	Ask someone if they know what a *-gooder is	Ask someone if anyone has * them a good turn today
Ask someone if they went to a * at the weekend	Ask someone if they like their steak well *	Ask someone if they have ever * up their house

---

CLOTHING DEPARTMENT

A You would like to buy a special outfit for your daughter's wedding. You go to the clothing department. You find a nice suit and ask to try it on.

CLOTHING DEPARTMENT

B You work in the clothing department. A woman comes in to buy a special outfit for her daughter's wedding. She asks to try it on and you show her the dressing rooms. You think it looks too tight and the color doesn't suit her. Tell her this politely.

ELECTRICAL APPLIANCE DEPARTMENT

A You bought an iPod from the Electrical Appliance department 6 weeks ago. The iPod worked for a while, but has now stopped working. Unfortunately you don't have the receipt anymore. Complain to the shop assistant and ask for a refund.

ELECTRICAL APPLIANCE DEPARTMENT

B You work in the Electrical Appliance department. A man complains about an iPod he bought 6 weeks ago. He asks for a refund, but he doesn't have a receipt and there is only one month guarantee. Tell him he can't have a refund.

SHOP TIL' YOU DROP • ROLE PLAY CARDS

FURNITURE DEPARTMENT

A You would like to buy a bed. You went to the furniture department yesterday and found one that you liked and it was in the sale. When you go to buy it today, the shop assistant says that the sale ended yesterday and the price has gone up. Complain a lot and ask for the sale price.

FURNITURE DEPARTMENT

B You work in the furniture department. A woman comes in and says she saw a bed advertised in the sale yesterday and she wants to buy it. Unfortunately the sale finished yesterday and the price has gone up today. She complains and is making quite a scandal. First, try to sell it for the normal price. Then, say that you are going to talk to the manager and see if you can sell it for the sale price.

STATIONERY DEPARTMENT

A You go the stationery department. You are looking for a birthday card for your husband. You would like a humorous one, but not too goofy. Ask the shop assistant for some advice.

STATIONERY DEPARTMENT

B You work in the stationery department. A woman wants to buy a birthday card for her husband. She wants a humorous one, but not goofy. There are many cards. Give her some advice.

SPORTS DEPARTMENT

A You go to the Sports department. You would like to take up golf, but don't know what kind of equipment you need for the sport. Ask the shop assistant for some help.

SPORTS DEPARTMENT

B You work in the Sports department. A man asks your advice about golf equipment. He is new to the sport. Show him the golf balls, clubs, tees and shoes. Try to sell him the lot.

KITCHENWARE DEPARTMENT

A You go to the Kitchenware department. You would like to buy a tea set for a friend's Golden wedding anniversary. You would like something very specific — eight cups, plates and saucers, as you know your friend has a big family.

KITCHENWARE DEPARTMENT

B You work in the kitchenware department. A woman would like to buy a tea set of 8 cups, plates and saucers. Unfortunately, you don't have eight, but you have six. Try and convince her to take the set of six.

BRITISH FOOD IS AWFUL – MYTH OR FACT?

BRITISH FOOD IS AWFUL – MYTH OR FACT?

A British food has a reputation all over the world for being tasteless, bland and greasy. Many foreigners who go to back to their countries after visiting Britain claim that they ate nothing but potatoes and overcooked vegetables while they were there. Is this reputation that Britain is the land of boring food really true?

B Let's look at two possible reasons behind this accusation. Firstly, during the second world war, many different kinds of foods were rationed, e.g. bananas, sugar and flour, which meant that many Europeans had to make do with what they had. Some of the older generation in Britain today can't stand seeing food wasted and cook just enough for their meal. Secondly, due to the cold weather, British people tend to eat more stodgy food consisting mainly of carbohydrates.

C However, nowadays British cuisine has really taken off with creative cooks such as Jamie Oliver and Nigella Lawson, who both have television programs. They tend to use fresh ingredients, as well as herbs and spices from different countries to produce delicious recipes. There is also a television program called *Ready, Steady, Cook* where 2 teams have to come up with a gourmet meal in a short time using limited ingredients.

D There is no doubt that immigrants in Britain have had an influence on British cooking, such as curry from India, Kebabs from Turkey and Chinese cooking. The British have learnt from other nations about different ingredients and are trying their hand at new recipes. All in all, I think that it is a myth to say that British food is awful nowadays as you can find delicious snacks and meals in many different restaurants and cafes all over Britain.

UNCOUNTABLE AND COUNTABLE NOUNS

Talk about how to make a favorite dish	Talk about something that has happened in the news recently	Talk about some advice you were given that you thought was very useful
Talk about some research you are working on or that you have done	Talk about how a piece of equipment works at home	Talk about your favorite music and a favorite song
Talk about something you have read recently which you found useful	Talk about the worst places for traffic in your city and offer some solutions	Talk about the progress you have made in English
Talk about a trip you went on recently	Talk about a problem you have had with your luggage	Talk about the advantages and disadvantages of the Internet
Talk about something you have recently learnt in your English course	Give the other students information about your hometown	Talk about a problem in your city and how you think it can be solved

ASK CARDS

ASK SOMEONE	**ASK SOMEONE**
To compare himself/herself with his/her brother/sister's height	To compare two famous buildings
ASK SOMEONE	**ASK SOMEONE**
About the best film he/she has ever seen	About the best book he/she has ever read
ASK SOMEONE	**ASK SOMEONE**
About the furthest place he/she has travelled to	About the most interesting person he/she has met
ASK SOMEONE	**ASK SOMEONE**
About the funniest english lesson he/she has ever had	The most expensive product they have ever bought
ASK SOMEONE	**ASK SOMEONE**
To compare learning english to his/her own language	To compare living in a city to living in the countryside
ASK SOMEONE	**ASK SOMEONE**
To compare two animals he/she likes	About the worst vacation he/she has ever had
ASK SOMEONE	**ASK SOMEONE**
About the most peaceful place they have ever been to	To compare driving a car to riding a bike
ASK SOMEONE	**ASK SOMEONE**
To compare two different countries	To compare two different regions in his/her country

ASK SOMEONE

About the most difficult exam he/she has ever taken

ASK SOMEONE

About the most expensive meal he/she has ever had

ASK SOMEONE

About the cheapest bargain he/she has ever found

ASK SOMEONE

About his/her earliest memory of school

TELL CARDS

TELL EVERYONE

About the oldest member of your family

TELL EVERYONE

About the most boring film you have ever seen

TELL EVERYONE

About the longest time you have ever been awake

TELL EVERYONE

About the nicest pub/bar to go to in your town

TELL EVERYONE

About the biggest challenge you have ever had

TELL EVERYONE

About the happiest day of your life

TELL EVERYONE

About the most delicious dish in your country

TELL EVERYONE

About the most generous person you have ever met

TELL EVERYONE

About a famous person you admire and one you don't admire and why

TELL EVERYONE

About two different famous geographical features in your country

COMPARATIVE AND SUPERLATIVE • TELL CARDS

TELL EVERYONE About the funniest joke you have ever heard	**TELL EVERYONE** About the worst job you could ever imagine
TELL EVERYONE About how the rich and the poor live in your country	**TELL EVERYONE** About the worst habit you can imagine someone having
TELL EVERYONE About the most exciting adventure you have ever had	**TELL EVERYONE** About the oldest building in your town
TELL EVERYONE About the most enjoyable party you have ever been to	**TELL EVERYONE** About the best site you have ever seen on the internet
TELL EVERYONE About the cleanest hotel you have ever been to	**TELL EVERYONE** About the youngest member of your family

OPTICAL ILLUSIONS

A • THE MEAN PUMPKIN

A strange event took place around Halloween time at Cornell University, Ithaca, the USA. When students woke up on an autumn morning, they saw a hollowed-out pumpkin in the McGraw's tower spire. There was a light flickering inside the pumpkin's mouth and the object looked mean and fierce.

The McGraw Tower was built at the end of the nineteenth century and there are 161 stairs to the top of the tower. At night, access to the stairs is cut off so nobody could possibly get to the top from the inside. As the tower is so high, it would be very dangerous from the outside. So, how exactly did this pumpkin get there?

There was a lot of hoo-ha about the happening for weeks to follow and some students and staff had debates about how the pumpkin got there. Each department had its own theory. The more superstitious thought it had been the act of witches, others produced a scientific explanation for the strange phenomenon.

B · CROP CIRCLES

The British media first reported seeing crop circles in the early 1980s. By 1990 crop circles had exploded into the public mind as the new phenomenon changed from simple circular patterns into huge and complex, geometric formations. The crop circles are a worldwide phenomenon and each year new reports come from an ever-increasing number of countries. However, the main concentration of events is to be found in Southern England, many around ancient sites such as Stonehenge, Avebury and Silbury Hill (the largest manmade mound in Europe).

Although there are many theories as to their creation, none have been able to explain satisfactorily exactly how the circles are made. However, perhaps some of the most persuasive evidence comes in the form of video taped footage showing small bright balls of white light in and around the crop circles. Other theories include the possibilities that hoaxers are responsible for the circles or even UFOs.

Fill in the gaps with the words from the box

INTRUDERS	ATTACK	FORCED
KNIFE	BREAKING INTO	DRUGS
RAISE THE ALARM	INJURIES	WAS ASSAULTED
WOODEN CLUB	FORENSIC TEAMS	
DISTRESSED	POLICE	

INTRUDERS AT WRONG HOUSE SAY SORRY

A young mother was recovering yesterday after two men armed with a _____ and a _____ broke into her bedroom at 2am, only to apologise and say that they had targeted the wrong house.

The pair then left quietly before _____ the woman's neighbors' and attacking a young man who was left with head _____.

An underworld feud or _____ quarrel are among motives being examined for the bizarre incident by South Yorkshire _____, who cordoned off the scene of the attack at Swinton, south Yorkshire yesterday. _____ are checking both properties while the woman, who has two small children, recovers from severe shock.

A spokesman for the police said that the men, wearing high visibility work vests _____ the back door to her house at 2am on Monday, and ran upstairs to the bedroom. One had the knife and the other the crude club made from a wooden plank.

"But it soon became obvious that the _____ had got the wrong address and they left, apologizing," said the spokesman. "No threats were made, although the woman was left in a _____ state."

The men then went next door in Station Street, close to the center of the small town near Rotherham, which is the hub of the remaining commercial waterway barge fleets in South Yorkshire. The spokesman said: "Inside the premises a 23-year old male _____ and required hospital treatment."

Other occupants fled unscathed to _____ and the attackers left hastily. Both were white and in their 20s and made no attempt to be inconspicuous in their reflective work vests. The woman was said to have been "absolutely terrified" at the time of the _____ but is making a good recovery.

DEPENDENT PREPOSITIONS

DEPENDENT PREPOSITIONS

Complete the sentences using the correct preposition

I am very interested _____ (leisure activity)

I am keen _____ (food/drink)

I was always very good _____ (school subject)

I am responsible _____ (job)

I have strong opinions _____ (something in the news)

I have great admiration _____ (a person) because

The last time I complimented (somebody) _____ (something) was when

I am excited _____ (something next week)

I am afraid _____ (animal)

My nationality is different _____ (another nationality) because

The smell of (smell) always reminds me _____

I am so tired _____ (something you do every day)

FOR AND AGAINST EXPRESSIONS

FOR	AGAINST
More diplomatic Yeah, I'd go along with you on that one. Yeah, exactly my thoughts too. Wow, really! I couldn't agree more. I feel exactly the same as you. Yeah, I didn't think of it like that, but you're right. Do you think so...? Yeah, I suppose you've got a point there.	**More diplomatic** Ok, I get your point, but... But if you were in my position, wouldn't you think the same? Everyone has got a point of view, but I still think... **Less diplomatic** Come on! I can't believe you're saying that! That is nonsense/rubbish! You've got to be joking!

FOR AND AGAINST EXPRESSIONS

FOR	AGAINST
More diplomatic Yeah, I'd go along with you on that one. Yeah, exactly my thoughts too. Wow, really! I couldn't agree more. I feel exactly the same as you. Yeah, I didn't think of it like that, but you're right. Do you think so...? Yeah, I suppose you've got a point there.	**More diplomatic** Ok, I get your point, but... But if you were in my position, wouldn't you think the same? Everyone has got a point of view, but I still think... **Less diplomatic** Come on! I can't believe you're saying that! That is nonsense/rubbish! You've got to be joking!

CONTROVERSIAL TOPICS

All couples should live together before getting married	Men and women are practically equal nowadays
Experiments carried out on animals should be banned	Prejudice against foreigners in my country has improved over the last ten years
Customer service in huge companies and big supermarkets should be improved	Video games and violent films should be banned for our children's sake
The government should pay for all education	Reality shows are like a human zoo and I have had enough of watching them
The Internet should be made available to everyone and the government should pay for it	The prison system in my country needs improving

ANY REGRETS, MR. PRESIDENT?

OPPOSITION TO THE PRESIDENT

Imagine that the President of your country for the last 4 years was not re-elected again. You do not support his party and did not re-elect him. Make a list with your partner of all the things you think he should not have done in his term in office. Think about health, education, agriculture, distribution of wealth, privatization, culture and the arts, unemployment, crime, foreign affairs, the economy, a scandal involving the President and anything else you wish to remember. Afterwards, present what you have discussed at a general meeting.

SUPPORTERS OF THE PRESIDENT

Imagine that the President of your country for the last 4 years was not re-elected again. You supported his party and are sad that he was not re-elected. Make a list with your partner of all the things you wish he had done better in his term in office. Think about health, education, agriculture, distribution of wealth, privatization, culture and the arts, unemployment, crime, foreign affairs, the economy, a scandal involving the President and anything else you wish to remember. Afterwards present what you have discussed at a general meeting.

ANY REGRETS, MR. PRESIDENT?

PRESIDENT AND FIRST LADY

You are the President and the First Lady. The President was in office for 4 years, but was not re-elected again. You are going to take part in a general meeting where there is a group of supporters and a group from the opposition. They are going to tell you what you shouldn't have done and what you could have done better. The topics they are discussing are: health, education, agriculture, distribution of wealth, privatization, culture and the arts, unemployment, crime, foreign affairs, the economy, a scandal involving you and anything else they wish to remember. You must be ready to defend yourselves, as you would not like to lose face in case of being re-elected in the future. Be assertive!

PUBS · ACTIVITY 1 AND 2

ACTIVITY 1

STUDENT A

1 What is a pub?
2 How old do you have to be to drink in a pub in the UK?
3 Are children allowed in pubs?
4 What time do pubs open and close in the UK?
5 What does it mean when the landlord/lady shouts "last orders"?

ACTIVITY 2

STUDENT B

1 Do you think you order drinks and food at the bar or at the table in a pub?
2 When do you pay for your drink?
3 Should you tip the barman/woman?
4 Can you smoke in a pub?
5 Can you play games in pubs?

ACTIVITY 1

STUDENT B

WHAT IS A PUB?

A pub (public house) is a place where alcoholic drinks can be bought and drunk and where food is often available.

DRINKING AGE IN THE UNITED KINGDOM

You can buy an alcoholic drink in the UK if you're over the age of 18. One word of advice — if you look young, you may be asked for identification.

FAMILIES

Some pubs allow families in for meals and some don't. Some even have areas where children can play, but they still require parents to supervise their offspring.

OPENING AND CLOSING TIMES

A law was recently passed for pubs to stay open 24 hours. It is up to each individual Landlord to apply for opening hours to suit his/her own establishment, so each pub can be different.

LAST ORDERS

Landlords/Landladies usually call "last orders" ten minutes before closing time and you can buy a drink up to closing time. "Last orders" is often indicated by ringing a bell and calling "last orders at the bar". When time is called, that's it — you can't buy booze to take home at this point.

ACTIVITY 2

STUDENT A

ORDERING DRINKS AND FOOD

Generally you order your drink from the bar and take it to where your friends are sitting/standing. You often order food from the bar too, although food will usually be brought to you after ordering. When you go to the bar to order a drink and if there's a group with you, don't all go together, there won't be room. One or two of you should go and order the drinks and bring them back.

PAYING FOR DRINKS

You usually pay for the drink when you order. The normal thing to do is to buy a round for everyone in your group. Afterwards someone will offer to buy the next round and so on.

TIPPING

If you feel someone in the pub has provided exceptional service you can offer to buy him or her a drink. Sometimes, he or she will actually take the drink (and drink it with you).

SMOKING

The whole of the United Kingdom became subject to a ban on smoking in enclosed public places in 2007.

GAMES

In some pubs you can play games such as darts, snooker, and shove ha' penny. You can also gamble on slot machines. Sometimes pubs organize general knowledge quizzes.

COMMON ERRORS • CARDS

Cook	Experience	Actual	Physician
Cooker	Experiment	Current	Sensible
Steal	History	Actually	Sensitive
Rob	Story	Presently	Borrow
Remember	Library	Nice	Lend
Remind	Bookshop	Sympathetic	Physicist
Hear	Parents	Teach	Prescription
Listen to	Relatives	Learn	Argue
Discuss	Recipe	Win	Dye

COMMON ERRORS

COMMON ERRORS
Circle the correct answer

1 The cook/cooker in this restaurant must be excellent. The food is superb.
2 Somebody stole/robbed my wallet. It was in my back pocket 10 minutes ago.
3 Can you remind/remember me to go to the bank. I have to get some money out the ATM.
4 Did you listen to/hear the news about that terrible tragedy? Those poor people!
5 She looks/looks like nice. I think I'm going to offer her a drink.
6 My neighbors are always discussing/arguing. It must be terrible for the kids.
7 My Granny has got white/grey hair. She painted/dyed it for many years, but now she's left it natural.
8 My scientific experiment/experience was a success. My supervisor was really pleased.
9 I used to love that history/story of Little Red Riding Hood. My Mum used to tell it to me.
10 I always go to the library/bookshop to lend/borrow a book for the weekend.

11 I have many relatives/parents all over the country, but I hardly ever see them.

12 The doctor gave me a recipe/prescription for some medicine.

13 My actual/current job is great. It is the best job I've ever had actually/presently.

14 The exhibition/exposition of Monet's famous masterpieces was absolutely amazing.

15 I have to take/pass an exam on Friday. I should get the results in 2 weeks' time.

16 My new teacher is so sympathetic/nice. In the first lesson she made such a good impression.

17 I have been teaching/learning foreign students for 6 years. It is such a rewarding job.

18 I won/got a fantastic present from my parents for Christmas. It was a brand new car!

19 I am a physicist/physician. My patients come to my surgery to be diagnosed.

20 My mum is so sensible/sensitive. She always cries when we go to the cinema.

Este livro foi impresso em janeiro de 2013
pela Yangraf Gráfica e Editora Ltda.,
sobre papel offset $90g/m^2$.